Also available in the EasiCoach™ Rugby Skills Activities Series

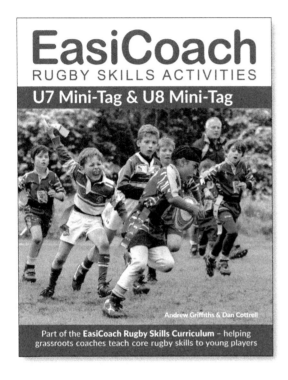

ISBN: 978-1-910338-39-1

Activities following the EasiCoach Rugby Curriculum for the age groups U7 Mini-Tag & U8 Mini-Tag, including handling, attacking and defending. By Andrew Griffiths and Dan Cottrell

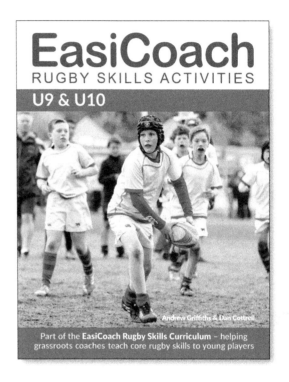

ISBN: 978-1-910338-40-7

Activities following the EasiCoach Rugby Curriculum for the age groups U9 & U10, introducing tackling and rucking and different types of passes. By Andrew Griffiths and Dan Cottrell

U11-U12 & U13-U16

EasiCoach
RUGBY SKILLS ACTIVITIES

U11-U12 & U13-U16

By Andrew Griffiths and Dan Cottrell

with thanks to Martin Skelton

First published in spiral bound and PDF editions in March 2015 by
Green Star Media Ltd
Meadow View House
Tannery Lane
Bramley
Guildford
Surrey
GU5 0AS

www.greenstarmedia.net

Second edition published August 2015

ISBN: 978-1-910338-41-4

For Green Star Media

Cover design: Matt Boulton
Photographs: Luke Ehrlanderr
Illustrations: Steve Thorpe, Artlife
Marketing: Haley Booth
Customer Services: Duncan Heard, Ben Hodges
Managing Director: Andrew Griffiths

Grateful thanks to London Irish RFC for permission to use the images in this book.

CONTENTS

U11-U12 Activities

CONTACT

DEFENCE

EVASION

HANDLING

KICKING

U13-U16 Activities

CONTACT

DEFENCE

EVASION

HANDLING

KICKING

INTRODUCTION

Welcome to EasiCoach™ Rugby Activities
– the parents' survival guide to coaching rugby

Dear Beginner Coach, Volunteer Dad or Mum, or "Roped-In" Helper,

If the world of rugby coaching seems a little daunting, don't worry, you are not alone! Like many parents involved in coaching their children:

- You volunteered to help, or were volunteered!
- You don't know much about rugby, or coaching
- You don't want to let the side down
- You want to do the best you can but don't have time to go on a course
- You're worried about coaching "the wrong thing".

EasiCoach provides ready-made, age appropriate, safe training activities, set out clearly on a single page, that even a child could understand. They are simple and easy to follow, and will make your life easier. EasiCoach covers ten age groups, available in three separate manuals:

- U7 & U8 Mini-Tag (31 activities)
- U9 & U10 (60 activities)
- U11-12 & U13-16 (60 activities)

How does this help you? EasiCoach coaching activities will help you to:

- Quickly understand what it is you're trying to achieve
- See what you need to do from just a few words and pictures
- Grasp the key dos and don'ts at a glance
- Check you have all the equipment you need (never more than basics)
- Cater for more or fewer players at your session
- Speak to your players with confidence

But here's what's really great about the EasiCoach approach. Follow all the materials in each manual, and your players will be learning the right skills for the right age group every season. They will be having more fun, and be on a gradual development pathway that should make them better, more skilful, players and continue playing rugby for longer.

Yours in rugby,

Andrew Griffiths

Dan Cottrell

GETTING STARTED

Your EasiCoach Activity Sheets

Each of the activity sheets in this manual covers a simple rugby skill appropriate for the U11-U12 age groups or for the U13-U16 age groups.

Remember, at these age groups some will have been playing rugby for many years – others may have just started, though newcomers at the older level become fewer.

Here's what you do to help all the players under your guidance.

- Read the notes below.

- In your 90 to 120 minute session, we suggest you run two or three activities from this book (depending on time), and then play a game.

- Use the illustration with each activity to show you (or your helpers) where to put the cones, balls and players in order to run the activity. (It's helpful if this can be done before the players arrive)

- Run a game.

You might hope not to have to get involved in refereeing, or "game coaching" as it is becoming known, or you might be dead keen to try. These days the objective is a free-flowing game, so (in training matches at least) the person with the whistle should act more as a helper than a referee. For competitive games at festivals and single matches, a qualified referee should be arranged.

The coaching, training, games or matches combined should last for no more than two hours at U11-U12 and at U13-U16.

Length of the session. At a typical training session, you should plan for no more than three EasiCoach activities each taking 25-30 minutes including setup and water breaks, followed by a game, for 40-50 minutes.

Setup. Arrive earlier than the players if you can, to set up the playing area for the chosen activities for the session. Set up two or three EasiCoach activities and be ready for the players to arrive.

Parents. Unless they are helping, parents are now recommended to stand at least 3m back from the edge of the pitch during training or matches. If space allows, your pitch set up should incorporate a cone or rope barrier to show parents where to stand. Encouragement of players is welcomed and criticism frowned upon.

No coaches on the pitch during matches. Adults should interfere as little as possible in the free flowing of the game at these levels.

Rules of Play

Throughout the world, rugby is changing at these age groups with new ideas being introduced wholesale or piecemeal. They are part of a debate about how and at what age to introduce elements of the high intensity adult game, and the trend is to delay the "full" game. Between the ages of U11 and U16, rugby authorities are and will be introducing new and amended rules covering when and how scrums, kicking, a free-for-all contact area (rucking and mauling) are introduced with accompanying new rules of play. In the absence of individual jurisdictions, they will do so at different speeds and with different outcomes. Inevitably, there will be adjustments and variations in different territories, so no broad skills guide written for a global audience can hope to cover all the ground and ongoing changes. The following are therefore guidelines based in broad principles being introduced by some of the main Northern hemisphere unions, which are either subject to change, or which may not be applicable to your rugby union. They are published as a guide only.

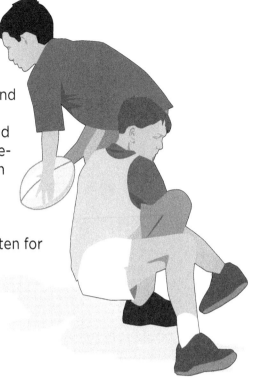

U11 Rugby

Number of players: 9v9 maximum. Rotate players on and off the field every few minutes so that no one is left out for very long and everyone gets substituted.

Maximum pitch size: 43m x 60m. Don't worry if you have not got this space – you can work with slightly smaller pitches if required with no problem. When the pitches are set up near goal posts, ensure that the posts have protective padding. If they are near corner or halfway marker flags, remove these before play starts.

Scrum: 3v3. The three players from each side nearest to the infringement take part in an uncontested scrum. The side putting the ball in wins.

Introduction of kicking. Kicking from hand is allowed but not kicking the ball in loose play – known as "fly-hacking". Defenders catching the ball can call "mark" anywhere on the pitch. If a defender knocks on from a kick, a scrum is awarded to the defending team.

Tackle contest. Competition for the ball is allowed in the tackle situation. Two players can compete for the tackle ball and two players can support the ball carrier.

No lineout or kicks for goal. Game is restarted with a free pass from lineout.

Ball size: 4

U12 Rugby

Number of players: 10v10. As with U11, rotate players on and off the field every few minutes so that no one is left out for very long and everyone gets substituted.

Pitch size: 43m x 60m

Scrum: 5v5. The five players from each side nearest to the infringement take part in an uncontested scrum. The side putting the ball in wins.

No lineout or kicks for goal. Game is restarted with a free pass from lineout.

Tackle contest: Unlimited numbers of players.

Ball size: 4

For older age groups, changes to suggested playing restrictions are limited and the game partly resembles the adult game, apart from the following:

U13 Rugby

Number of players: 13v13. If you have more numbers, ensure regular rotation and substitution.

Scrum: 6v6. Contested. Hooker strikes, and scrum can push. Players must be trained and volunteer to play in the scrum.

Kicking: Kicking loose ball allowed.

No lineout or kicks for goal. Game is restarted with a free pass from lineout.

Pitch size: 60m x 90m

Ball size: 4

U14 Rugby

Number of players: 15v15.

Scrum: 8v8. Contested. Hooker strikes, and scrum can push. Players must be trained and volunteer to play in the scrum.

Introduction of uncontested lineout (no lifting) and kicking at goal.

Pitch size: 70m x 100m

Ball size: 4

U15 Rugby

Number of players: 15v15.

Scrum: 8v8. Contested. Hooker strikes, and scrum can push. Players must be trained and volunteer to play in the scrum.

Pitch size: Full size

Ball size: 5

U16 Rugby

Number of players: 15v15.

Introduction of lineout lifting.

Pitch size: Full size

Ball size: 5

A 1-2-3 of Coaching Children

1. Use the 30 Second Rule
The 30 second rule works because children learn best by doing, not listening, and 30 seconds is about as much as most of them can take. So, with that in mind, let them do as much as possible and listen as little as possible. After 30 seconds, many of your audience will have stopped listening anyway, and very little if any of what you go on to say will be heard, let alone understood.

Only having 30 seconds to talk can make life easier if you are privately anxious about speaking, or concerned about saying the wrong thing, as it reduces the chance of making a mistake. Being time limited forces you to think carefully beforehand about what you are going to say. The outcome should be reduced waffle and getting to the point more quickly. Children like this simplicity. It is also worth bearing in mind that in chillier climates, players will get cold very quickly if they are standing round listening to you for more than a short period.

Just 30 seconds really only gives you the chance to pick up one point from the activity the players have been doing. While you are observing them, think about what you want to say. This can be praise or encouragement, or it can be to offer a suggestion to a common problem that is occurring. Use your 30 seconds to laser in on just one. That single message is far more likely to get through if it is on its own.

One trick to increase attention levels is to get young players as attentive as possible before you start talking, simply by asking them to be quiet, or standing silently waiting for them to quiet down. The rule is not always practical, though. Sometimes, when you are introducing something new, you will have to talk to the players for longer. In these situations, make sure you involve the players either by asking questions, giving them a break from your voice – or by getting volunteers to demonstrate. But if you can do it in 30 seconds – congratulations!

2. When and how to correct mistakes
If a young player is making a mistake, we feel duty bound to do something about it. However, we shouldn't always step in. Young people learn from their mistakes by themselves and from feedback from their peers. They don't want or need an adult telling them every time they don't get something right, or as good as it should be – they know!

You may notice as your start coaching young children that youngsters can be intimidated by corrections. The action of correcting can be counterproductive in itself, with some players not taking on board what they need to change.

There are some things that we must correct. Anything that can harm the player or someone else, such as kicking, punching, verbal abuse or any other sort of foul play. These are non-negotiable. Do not hesitate to blow the whistle to stop play and highlight the actions of the offender, so that everyone is aware of the issue and can learn.

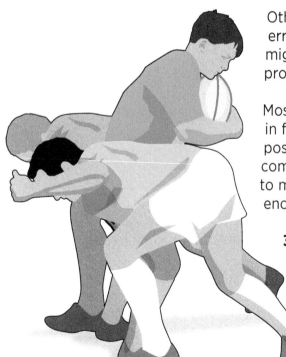

Other areas we might correct are discretionary. Technical errors, such as poor hand positioning on the ball. More difficult might be decision-making errors such as wrong options. This is problematic because there are often a number of options.

Most people don't like criticism or corrections at all, let alone in front of others, and children are no different. If at all possible, take the player aside on a one-to-one basis to make a comment. If parents are nearby, you might feel it is appropriate to make the point in their presence. One or two words may be enough, but the key is to "talk" and not raise your voice.

3. Coach by gentle questioning
Research shows that learning comes from self-discovery. This means players realise how to solve problems and react to situations by finding their own solutions. Coaches should try to reduce the amount of time they spend "telling" the players what to do. Instead, through questioning, they should look to empower their players.

To aid good learning the coach needs to communicate well verbally. The choice of words is often not as important as the way they are told. Remember:

- Don't use jargon or sarcasm.
- Promote positive comments.
- Back up criticism with a way forward.
- Keep sentences short.
- Don't make too many points.
- Summarise at the end – some players may not have understood the first time around.

Gentle questioning

Asking questions is useful because it:

- Gains the attention of the players.
- Lets the coach learn what the players know.
- Involves the players in the learning process.
- Allows the players to express their opinions.
- Helps the coach check for understanding.

Asking the best questions

- Use open questions – questions that cannot be answered with just "yes" or "no". Start questions with words, like "what", "how" or "where".
- Don't use "why", because it can be construed as negative.
- Wait for the answer, don't hurry the player.
- Listen, don't anticipate the answer. Try not to rephrase the answer once given.

When to "tell" and when to "question"

Tell when:

- You have a short period of time to get your point across.
- Specific instructions are needed. For instance, health and safety issues or laws of the game.
- A larger group makes question and answer sessions unwieldy.

Question to:

- Check your players' understanding.
- Gain feedback.
- Improve your players' learning.

USING YOUR EASICOACH ACTIVITIES

6 STEPS TO EASICOACH SUCCESS

1. Find the activity you need
2. Look at the pictures and read the text
3. Check what equipment you'll need when you get to the club
4. Take the book to training
5. Set up your activity
6. EasiCoach it!

The age group the activity has been written for along with the skills category that the activity belongs to and its place in that category

The title tells you the skill that the players will develop by doing this activity

The name of the activity – you can tell this to your players: "Today we're going to play..."

'Call out' gives you some key phrases to tell your players as they do the activity, to help them understand what they should be doing and how they should be doing it

Each activity is explained simply and clearly, step by step

The diagrams show you what the activity should look like on the pitch. There might be one, two or three diagrams – whatever makes it easiest for you to understand

Detailed illustrations show how the skills should be performed

The key helps you understand the diagram – which way the players are running and where the ball is going

'How many players do I need' tells you how you can adapt the activity if you have more players than are shown

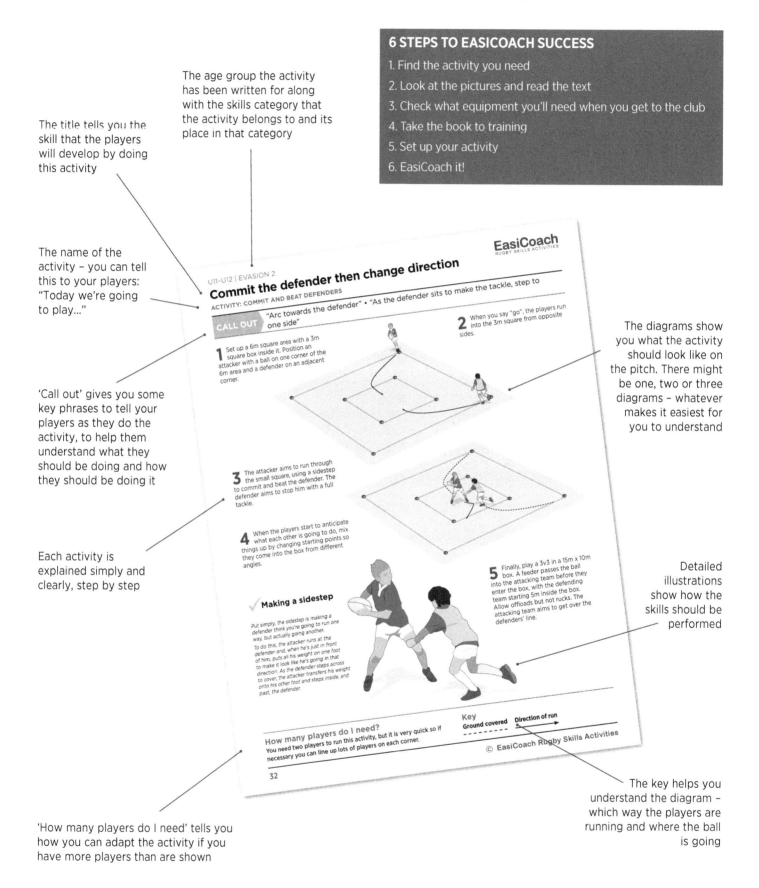

EasiCoach
RUGBY SKILLS ACTIVITIES

U11-U12 | EVASION 2
Commit the defender then change direction
ACTIVITY: COMMIT AND BEAT DEFENDERS

CALL OUT "Arc towards the defender" • "As the defender sits to make the tackle, step to one side"

1 Set up a 6m square area with a 3m square box inside it. Position an attacker with a ball on one corner of the 6m area and a defender on an adjacent corner.

2 When you say "go", the players run into the 3m square from opposite sides.

3 The attacker aims to run through the small square, using a sidestep to commit and beat the defender. The defender aims to stop him with a full tackle.

4 When the players start to anticipate what each other is going to do, mix things up by changing starting points so they come into the box from different angles.

5 Finally, play a 3v3 in a 15m x 10m box. A feeder passes the ball into the attacking team before they enter the box, with the defending team starting 5m inside the box. Allow offloads but not rucks. The attacking team aims to get over the defenders' line.

✓ **Making a sidestep**

Put simply, the sidestep is making a defender think you're going to run one way, but actually going another.

To do this, the attacker runs at the defender and, when he's just in front of him, puts all his weight on one foot to make it look like he's going in that direction. As the defender steps across to cover, the attacker transfers his weight onto his other foot and steps inside, and past, the defender.

How many players do I need?
You need two players to run this activity, but it is very quick so if necessary you can line up lots of players on each corner.

Key
Ground covered   Direction of run
- - - - - - - - -

© EasiCoach Rugby Skills Activities

32

U11-U12
CONTACT

Change position to improve ball placement

ACTIVITY: RUCK PLACEMENT

CALL OUT "Stretch to get the ball back" • "Roll the shoulders to help to get more control of the contact contest"

1 Set up a 3m square area and number each side from 1 to 4. Put an attacker with a ball and a defender in the centre of the area.

The attacker holds the ball while the defender places his hands on the attacker's shoulders

2 When you say "go", the defender puts his hands on the shoulders of the attacker.

The attacker must be thinking about where the ball must go after he is tackled and what he has to do to get it to that point

3 You then call out one of the four sides of the square (in this case "2") and the defender tries to wrestle the attacker to the ground.

4 The attacker fights to stay on his feet but when grounded, he must push the ball back towards the side called out.

5 Develop by having one ball carrier at one end of the box against two defenders. He aims to get to the far end but must aim to present the ball back to his own try line if he is tackled.

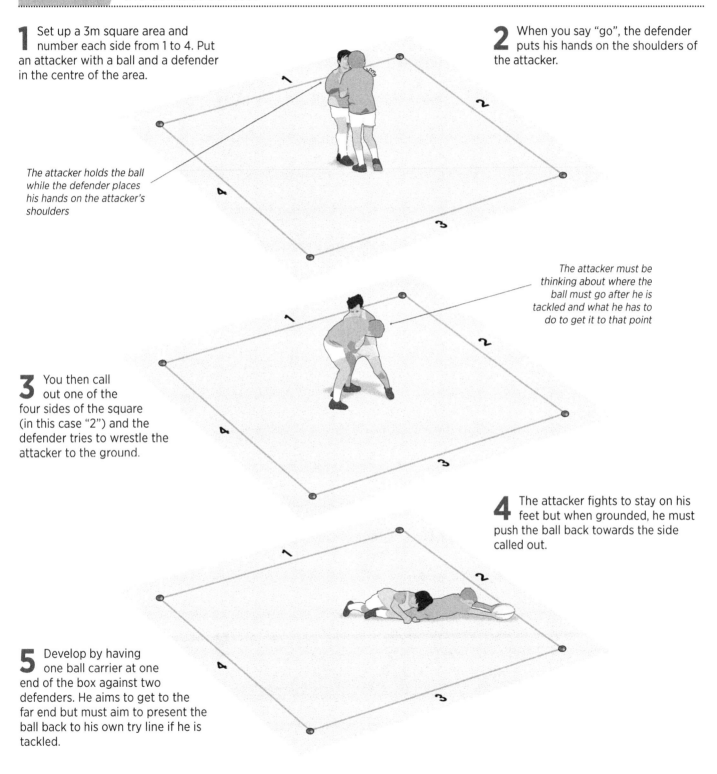

How many players do I need?
Run this activity with as many pairs of players as you have room (and balls) for.

Key

Manage the ball in contact and win the collision

ACTIVITY: ABC: AGILITY BEFORE CONTACT

EasiCoach
RUGBY SKILLS ACTIVITIES

CALL OUT "Take short steps to stay balanced" • "Keep the ball away from the defender" • "Keep moving forward if you can"

1 Set out a 3m square area. Put an attacker and defender facing each other on opposite sides of the area and a feeder on one side of the area.

Because the area is small, there is no real opportunity for the attacker to get up any speed, so he will have to use short steps to move to the side of the defender (he might step left and then right for instance)

2 When you say "go", the feeder passes the ball to the attacker who attempts to get to the opposite side of the area. If he is tackled, he must present the ball properly.

3 Move the game on by having the attacker facing away from the defender before turning to receive the ball. This means he will have to react quicker to avoid the defender.

4 Finally, move to the 5m x 3m area and put two attackers against two defenders with a feeder at the side.

5 When you say "go", the feeder can pass to either of the attackers. The attacker then tries to get to the far end. He can pass, offload or be driven forward by his team mate.

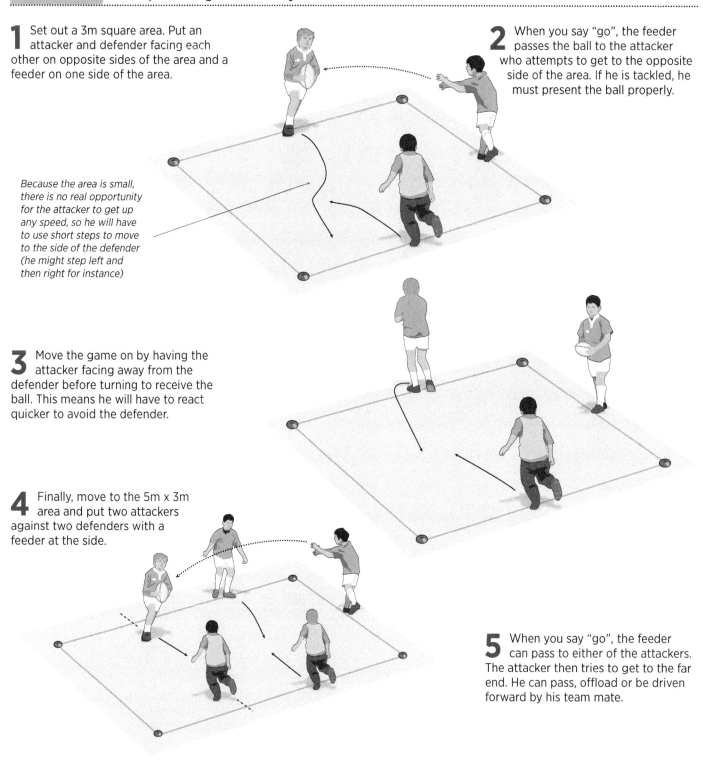

How many players do I need?
You need three players to start with and then five. With more players, set up more squares alongside.

Key
Ground covered	Pass	Direction of run
– – – – – –	·········▸	——————▶

© **EasiCoach Rugby Skills Activities**

Drive the ball carrier forward in a maul

ACTIVITY: MAUL BASICS

EasiCoach
RUGBY SKILLS ACTIVITIES

"Keep the ball from the defender" • "Drive forward with short steps"

1 Mark out a 5m square area. Inside the area put a defender with a ball-carrying attacker 1m in front of him and two more attackers just behind the ball carrier.

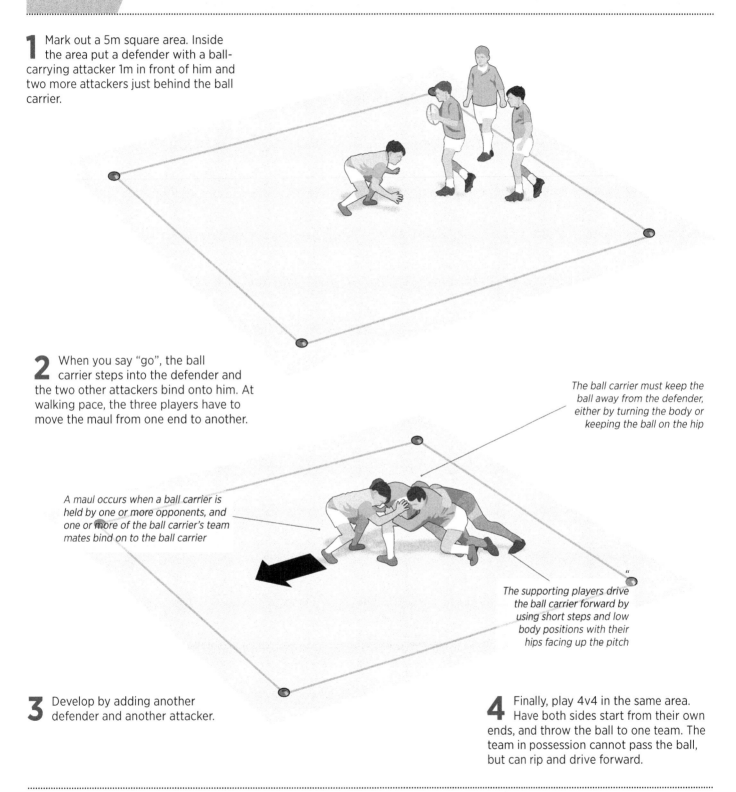

2 When you say "go", the ball carrier steps into the defender and the two other attackers bind onto him. At walking pace, the three players have to move the maul from one end to another.

The ball carrier must keep the ball away from the defender, either by turning the body or keeping the ball on the hip

A maul occurs when a ball carrier is held by one or more opponents, and one or more of the ball carrier's team mates bind on to the ball carrier

The supporting players drive the ball carrier forward by using short steps and low body positions with their hips facing up the pitch

3 Develop by adding another defender and another attacker.

4 Finally, play 4v4 in the same area. Have both sides start from their own ends, and throw the ball to one team. The team in possession cannot pass the ball, but can rip and drive forward.

How many players do I need?
Run this activity with four players. Set up more squares and get lots of fours practising mauling. Make sure players try out all the roles.

Key
Direction of run
———————➤

Tell the ball carrier his options going into contact

ACTIVITY: COMMUNICATION INTO CONTACT

CALL OUT "Be clear and concise with your call" • "Don't get too close to the ball carrier until he makes contact – then weigh up your options"

1 Mark out a 6m x 3m area. Put a defender in the middle of the area and a ball carrier and a support player at one end of the area.

2 When you say "go", the ball carrier runs at the defender with the support player just behind.

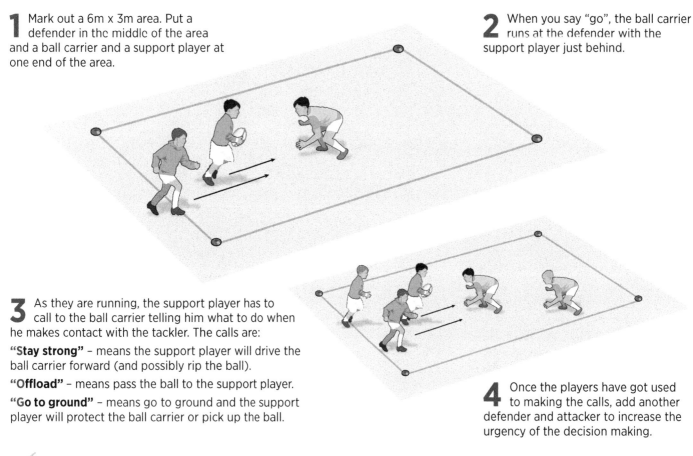

3 As they are running, the support player has to call to the ball carrier telling him what to do when he makes contact with the tackler. The calls are:

"Stay strong" – means the support player will drive the ball carrier forward (and possibly rip the ball).

"Offload" – means pass the ball to the support player.

"Go to ground" – means go to ground and the support player will protect the ball carrier or pick up the ball.

4 Once the players have got used to making the calls, add another defender and attacker to increase the urgency of the decision making.

✓ **Making the right call**

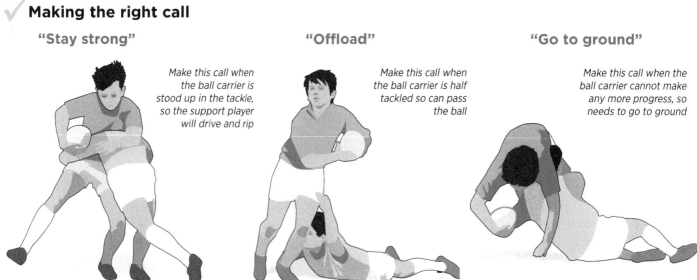

"Stay strong"	"Offload"	"Go to ground"
Make this call when the ball carrier is stood up in the tackle, so the support player will drive and rip	*Make this call when the ball carrier is half tackled so can pass the ball*	*Make this call when the ball carrier cannot make any more progress, so needs to go to ground*

How many players do I need?
You need three players to start the activity and then add in two more. With more players, line up attackers ready to take their turn.

Key
Direction of run
⟶

Tackle when off balance

ACTIVITY: DRIVE, RUCK, SUPPORT

CALL OUT "Stay on your feet in the tackle contest" • "Keep driving over the ball" •
"Move quickly to support the tackle"

1 Mark out a 5m x 2m box with a 2m x 3m box alongside. Put an attacker with a ball and a defender opposite each other in the smaller box, and two attackers opposite two ruck pad holders in the larger box.

2 When you say "go", the attacker with the ball aims to get past the defender to the other side of his box, and the two other attackers drive into the two ruck pad holders in the larger box.

3 The two attackers drive the pads back out of their box while the defender tackles and brings down the ball carrier (the ball carrier should allow himself to be tackled).

The ball carrier must stay strong in the tackle to give supporters a chance to get there

4 Once they have been driven back, the ruck pad holders drop their pads and all four players run to support the tackle contest.

Support players must be quick to the situation and make sure they square up to come through the tackle gate from the front

5 Continue until the ball is clearly won by either side, or an infringement occurs. Rotate players after each go.

How many players do I need?
You need six players to run the activity. With more players, maintain a steady flow through the activity.

Key

Ground covered — — — — —

Direction of run ⟶

Keep the ball available to be ripped or passed

ACTIVITY: KEEP THE BALL ALIVE IN CONTACT

CALL OUT "Stay on your feet" • "Take small, fast steps through the contact area"

1 Set up a 5m square area. Put two attackers, one with a ball, on one side of the area (one on each corner) and two ruck pad holders together in the centre on the other side.

2 When you say "go", the ball carrier runs at one of the ruck pad holders and, in the last 2m, passes to the other attacker who runs on to the ball at pace and tries to smash between the two ruck pad holders.

3 Players attack and defend in different partnerships, in 30-second sets.

The supporting player runs faster than the ball carrier to create momentum and get past his team mate when the contact area is reached

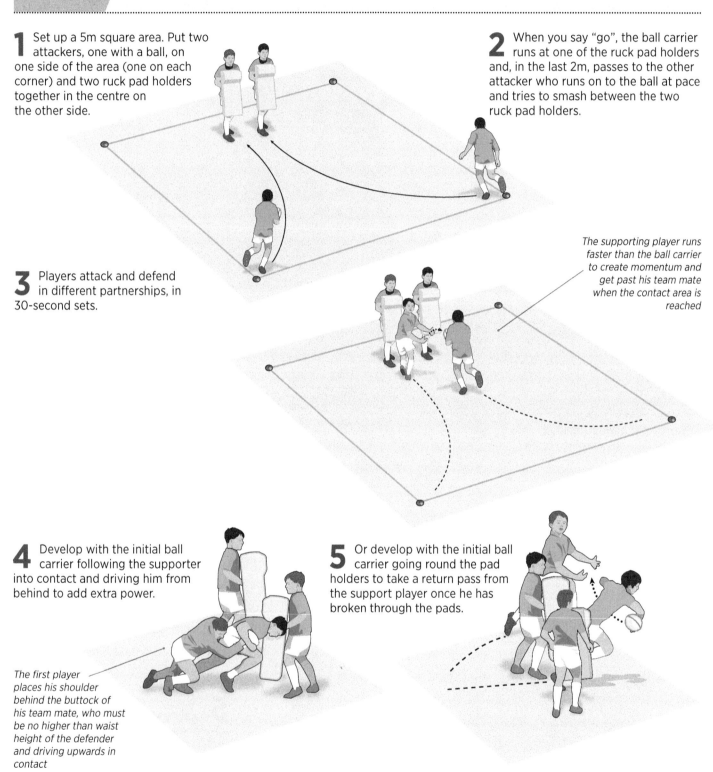

4 Develop with the initial ball carrier following the supporter into contact and driving him from behind to add extra power.

The first player places his shoulder behind the buttock of his team mate, who must be no higher than waist height of the defender and driving upwards in contact

5 Or develop with the initial ball carrier going round the pad holders to take a return pass from the support player once he has broken through the pads.

How many players do I need?
You need four players. With more, line up attacking players on the two corners so they can run through the activity quickly.

Key

Ground covered	Pass	Direction of run
- - - - -	·······▶	——▶

Support and drive a maul

ACTIVITY: SUPPORT THE MAUL

CALL OUT "Roll the upper body to make yourself more difficult to hold onto" • "Support player, tell the ball carrier what to do – stay on your feet, drive, my ball, go to ground"

1 Mark out a 5m square area using different coloured cones on each corner. Put a ball carrier and defender back-to-back about 1m apart in the area. Another attacker faces the ball carrier outside the square.

2 Shout which cone the ball carrier should attack, here "blue". He turns and goes for that cone.

3 The defender tries to stop him either by grabbing the ball or tackling. The support player joins the contact situation.

4 The ball carrier cannot offload the ball but can have it ripped off him.

5 Play until the ball is lost, a tackle is completed and the support player has protected the ball or the ball carrier goes over the cone.

6 Develop by adding another defender. He and the support attacker run around the cones in front of them after you call a colour.

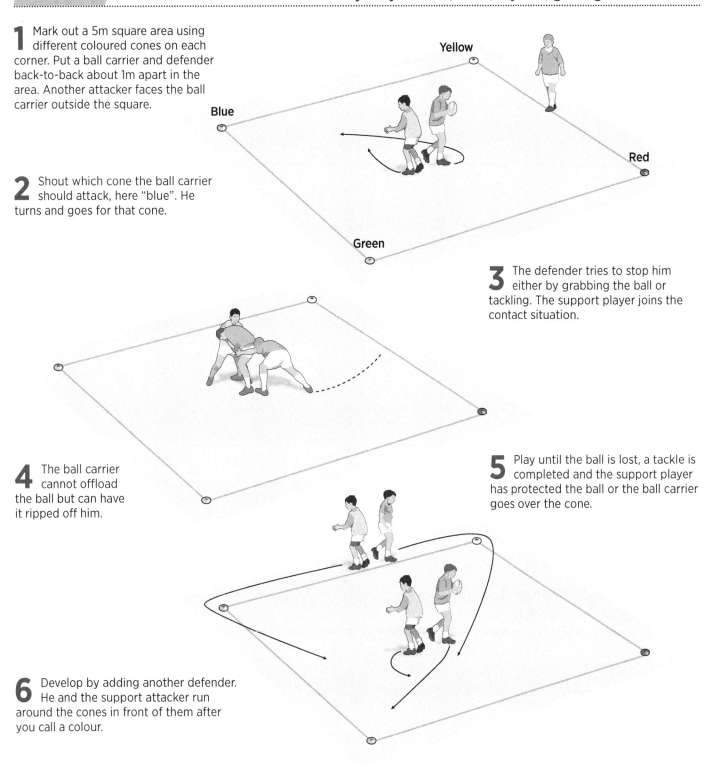

How many players do I need?
You need three players to begin the activity, then add a fourth. With more players, mark out more 5m areas.

Key

Ground covered	Direction of run
- - - - - - -	⟶

Power step into the defender and present the ball

ACTIVITY: POWER STEPPING

CALL OUT "Ball carrier accelerates towards the defender" • "Power step down low, then up and through the defender" • "Support players stay close at all times"

✓ Practising the power step

The attacker accelerates into contact with a low body position...

... power steps back the defender from square on...

... then, with the contact collision won, assesses his next move

1 Split your players into groups of four. A defender holds a ruck pad. Two attackers (1 and 2) start 5m away with a third attacker (3) 5m behind the defender.

2 When you say "go", attacker 1 runs with the ball and power steps into the pad knocking the defender back. He pops the ball to attacker 2 who runs to attacker 3.

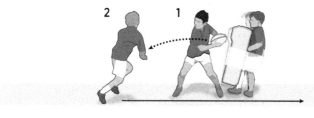

3 The defender turns around, allowing attacker 2 to run towards him, power step and pop to attacker 3. Each player carries three times and then they swap the defender.

✓ Using the power step in a match situation

Players must power step into contact...

... turn and present the ball to the support player who must be close behind...

How many players do I need?
You need four players to run this activity. If you have more players, get more groups of four working on their power stepping.

Key

Ground covered	Pass	Direction of run
– – – – – – –	·······▶	——▶

U11-U12
DEFENCE

Tackle with the head tight to the ball carrier

ACTIVITY: TACKLING LOW AND HARD

CALL OUT "Keep your eyes open in the tackle" • "Get your foot close to ball carrier" • "Get a tight grip"

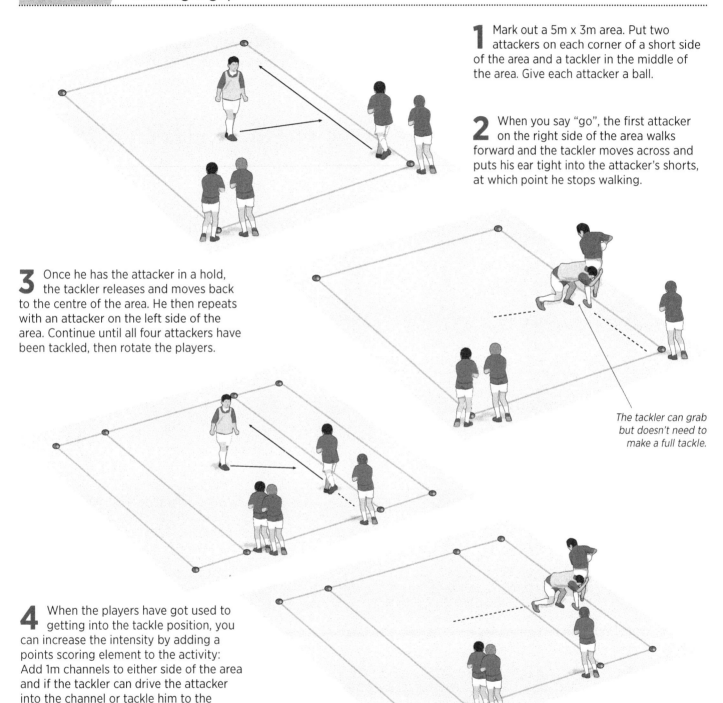

1 Mark out a 5m x 3m area. Put two attackers on each corner of a short side of the area and a tackler in the middle of the area. Give each attacker a ball.

2 When you say "go", the first attacker on the right side of the area walks forward and the tackler moves across and puts his ear tight into the attacker's shorts, at which point he stops walking.

3 Once he has the attacker in a hold, the tackler releases and moves back to the centre of the area. He then repeats with an attacker on the left side of the area. Continue until all four attackers have been tackled, then rotate the players.

The tackler can grab but doesn't need to make a full tackle.

4 When the players have got used to getting into the tackle position, you can increase the intensity by adding a points scoring element to the activity: Add 1m channels to either side of the area and if the tackler can drive the attacker into the channel or tackle him to the ground, he scores a point.

How many players do I need?

You need at least five players, but with more you can line up attackers and rotate the tackler frequently.

Key

Ground covered   **Direction of run**

- - - - - - - -   →

Get feet close to the ball carrier when tackling

ACTIVITY: STEP IN AND TACKLE

EasiCoach
RUGBY SKILLS ACTIVITIES

CALL OUT "Keep your feet active" • "Eyes fixed on the tackle target at all times" • "Step into the tackle"

1 Set out 12 cones in a large X shape with a 1m box in the middle.

2 Put a tackler on one side of the 1m box and a ball carrier on the other side, facing him.

3 On your signal, the ball carrier moves to one of the cones to the side of him (you indicate left or right) and runs straight for the cone in front of him. The tackler moves forward and to the side to make a side-on tackle.

4 Repeat the exercise four times, moving to both left and right cones. Once the players are confident working from the 1m cones, move the ball carrier back to the middle cones cones and repeat. Finally, move him back to the end cones. The tackler always starts from the 1m box.

5 Swap roles and repeat in the opposite direction.

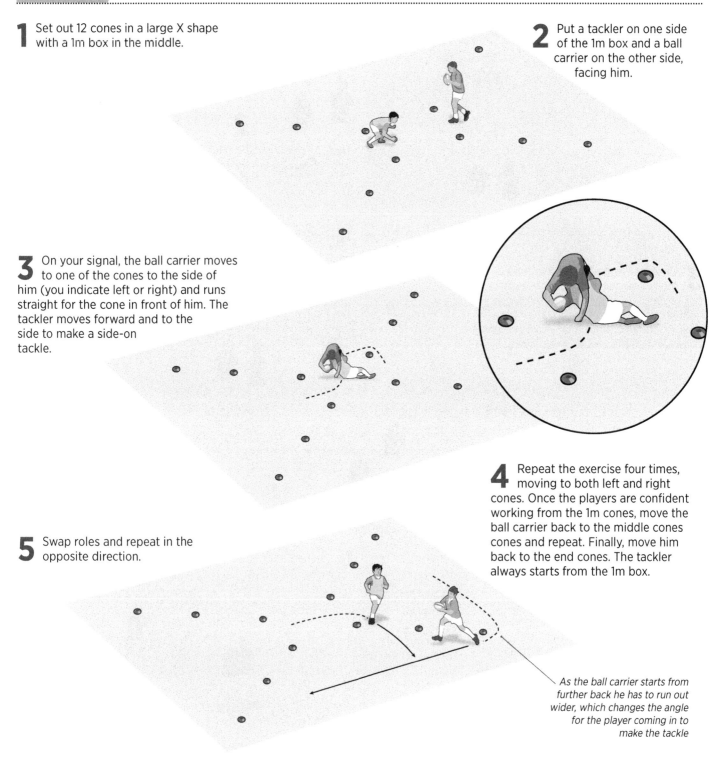

As the ball carrier starts from further back he has to run out wider, which changes the angle for the player coming in to make the tackle

How many players do I need?
Get your players into pairs. Either set up lots of X-shaped areas, or get the pairs swapping in and out frequently.

Key

Ground covered | Direction of run
- - - - - - - - | ⟶

© **EasiCoach Rugby Skills Activities**

Engage with the shoulder and drive in the tackle

ACTIVITY: TACKLE AT THE RIGHT HEIGHT

| **CALL OUT** | "Sight the target area early" • "Close down the space quickly" |

1 Set up a 10m square area with 1m coned gates in the centre at both ends. Put an attacker and a defender in the middle of the area by a red cone, facing their own coned gates. Place a blue cone 3m to one side of the red cone and a green cone 3m to the other side.

2 On your call of "go", the players run to their gate and then back towards the middle. As they begin their return, you call a colour cone, here "green". The attacker runs to that cone and then aims to continue across the area to score, while the defender aims to tackle him side-on and low at the cone.

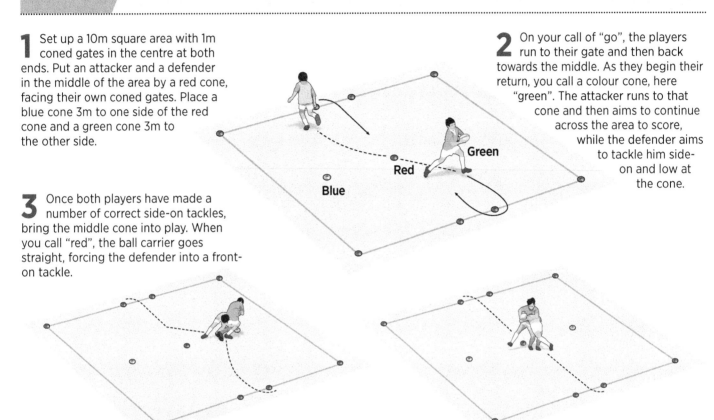

3 Once both players have made a number of correct side-on tackles, bring the middle cone into play. When you call "red", the ball carrier goes straight, forcing the defender into a front-on tackle.

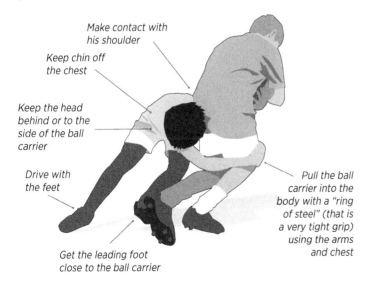

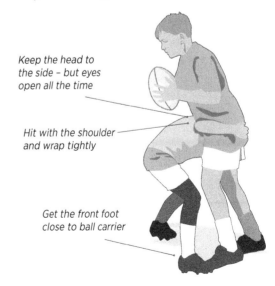

✓ Making a side-on tackle

Make contact with his shoulder

Keep chin off the chest

Keep the head behind or to the side of the ball carrier

Drive with the feet

Get the leading foot close to the ball carrier

Pull the ball carrier into the body with a "ring of steel" (that is a very tight grip) using the arms and chest

✓ Making a front-on tackle

Keep the head to the side – but eyes open all the time

Hit with the shoulder and wrap tightly

Get the front foot close to ball carrier

How many players do I need?
Start with two players, but line up others ready for their go – let them watch and learn from each other's mistakes.

Key

Ground covered	Direction of run
- - - - - - -	→

Get low to make a chop tackle

ACTIVITY: THE CHOP TACKLE

CALL OUT "Get close to the ball carrier" • "Get low and accelerate into the ball carrier's legs"

1 Split players into pairs, an attacker and a defender, with one ball per pair. Line attackers up on one side of the 10m square area and defenders on an adjacent side (not opposite).

2 When you say "go", the attacker aims to run through the square and score at the far end. The defender's job is to stop him using a low chop tackle.

3 Begin at jogging pace and build up to full speed. Once mastered, encourage the tackler to get to his feet and challenge for the ball.

4 When players are confident making a chop tackle, Introduce a support player with a ruck pad to make challenging for the ball after the tackle more realistic. Add a second defender to also challenge for the ball.

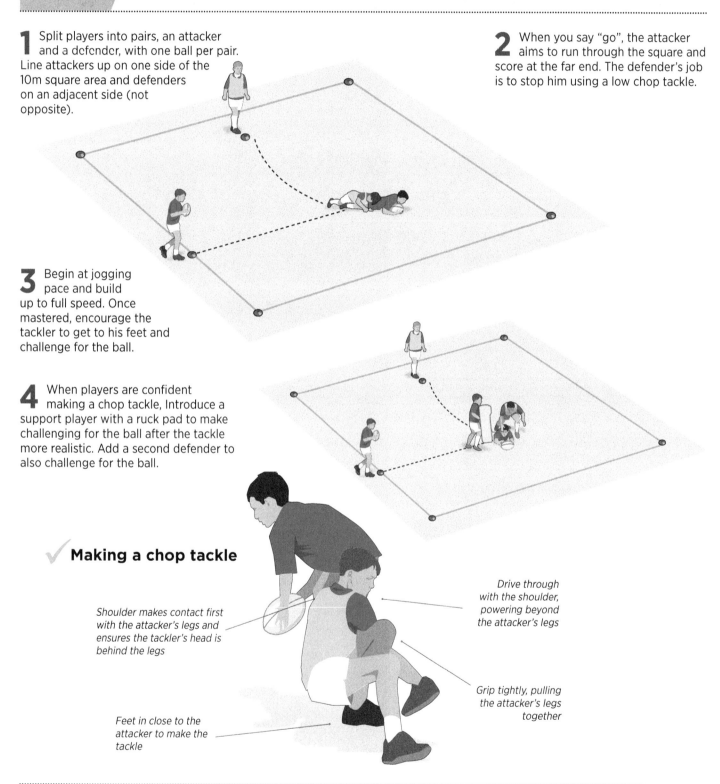

✓ Making a chop tackle

Shoulder makes contact first with the attacker's legs and ensures the tackler's head is behind the legs

Drive through with the shoulder, powering beyond the attacker's legs

Grip tightly, pulling the attacker's legs together

Feet in close to the attacker to make the tackle

How many players do I need?

Put your players into pairs – one attacker and one defender – and line them up ready to take their turn.

Key
Ground covered
- - - - - - - -

© **EasiCoach Rugby Skills Activities**

Roll away from a tackle and get back in the game

EasiCoach
RUGBY SKILLS ACTIVITIES

ACTIVITY: BOUNCE AND RELOAD FROM THE TACKLE

CALL OUT "Use a low tackle to get the player to ground" • "Bounce up onto your feet quickly" • "Show you have released the tackled player before going for the ball again"

1 Split players into pairs and make one of each pair an attacker and the other a defender. The defender kneels down on one knee – the knee opposite to the shoulder he will tackle with The attacker has a ball and starts 2m away.

If the defender kneels on his right knee, as here, he will tackle with his left shoulder

2 When you say "go", the attacker runs at the defender, who makes a low tackle, driving off his foot and gripping hard.

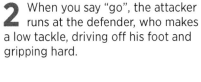

3 Once he has completed the low tackle, he rolls out and away, bouncing up on to his feet quickly.

4 Add another attacker and defender 5m away who compete over the ball and help the tackler gain an added sense of how he can affect the tackle contest.

How many players do I need?
Start with two players and then move to four. With more, put them into pairs and give them enough space to practise the activity.

Key

Ground covered   **Direction of run**

- - - - - - -   ⟶

Get up and challenge for the ball after a tackle

ACTIVITY: TACKLE, UP AND CHALLENGE

CALL OUT "Make a low tackle" • "Get back to your feet as quickly as possible" • "Get hands on the ball before support arrives"

1 Set out a line of three cones each 1m apart and another similar line of cones 5m away, forming a channel. Place a single cone 5m behind the end cone of one of the lines

2 Start with a ball carrier on the middle cone of one of the lines and a defender on the middle cone of the other line. An attacking support player starts on the cone 5m back.

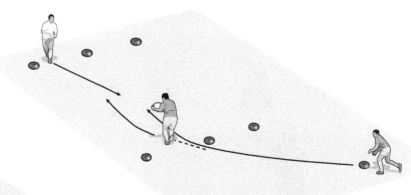

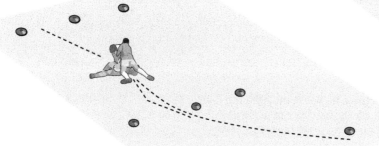

3 When you say "go", the ball carrier starts running (or jogging depending on the intensity) and tries to beat the defender and score over the opposite line. At the same time, the support player runs round the middle cone before entering the channel.

4 The defender moves forward and makes the tackle. His aim is to get back to his feet and get his hands on the ball before the support player arrives and touches him.

✓ Getting back on the feet after making a tackle

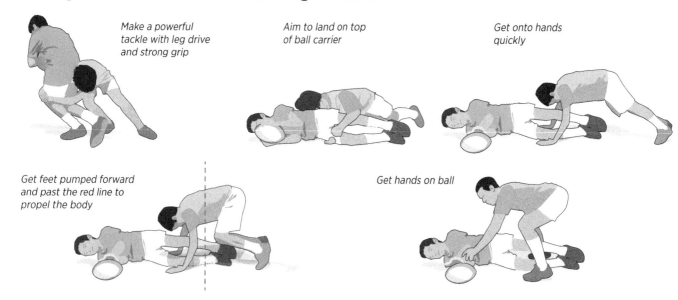

Make a powerful tackle with leg drive and strong grip

Aim to land on top of ball carrier

Get onto hands quickly

Get feet pumped forward and past the red line to propel the body

Get hands on ball

How many players do I need?
Split your players into threes and get them moving quickly through the channel. Rotate the roles.

Key

Ground covered   Direction of run

- - - - - - -   ⟶

Defend 1v1 and as part of a group

EasiCoach
RUGBY SKILLS ACTIVITIES

ACTIVITY: DEFEND AS UNITS

CALL OUT "Call to say who you are marking" • "Come forward in defence but stay balanced and be ready to move to the side"

1 Mark out a 10m square area with a 1m square box in the middle. Put a pair of attackers on one side of the area and a pair of defenders on the opposite side, and put a ball in the 1m box.

2 When you say "go", both pairs come forward. One attacker goes to the ball and crouches over it. The other attacker goes to one side. One defender stands outside the box opposite the ball carrier, and the other marks the other attacker. At this point, the defenders must stay on their side of the box.

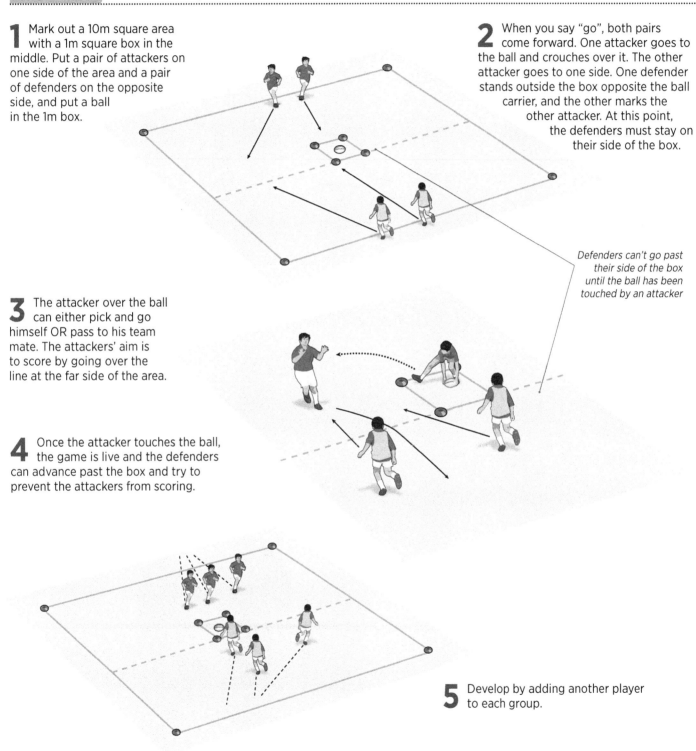

Defenders can't go past their side of the box until the ball has been touched by an attacker

3 The attacker over the ball can either pick and go himself OR pass to his team mate. The attackers' aim is to score by going over the line at the far side of the area.

4 Once the attacker touches the ball, the game is live and the defenders can advance past the box and try to prevent the attackers from scoring.

5 Develop by adding another player to each group.

How many players do I need?
You need four players for the first part of the activity and two more for the development.

Key

Ground covered	Pass	Direction of run
– – – – – – –	·····················▸	⟶

Get close and drive through the tackle

ACTIVITY: THE DRIVING TACKLE

CALL OUT "Get a tight grip with your arms" • "Get your head in close and on the correct side" • "Drive the attacker back one step"

1 Set up: In pairs on the try line. The attacker faces the defender with his arms folded across his stomach at arm's length from a tackler.

2 On your call, the tackler, quickly steps forward, makes impact under the arm pits or lower, wraps his arms around the target and drives him back one step.

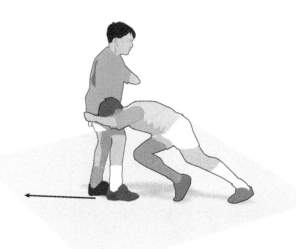

3 Repeat five times before swapping over.

4 Once the players have got used to the routine, stand the defender on the try line and the attacker on the 5m line. On your first call, the attacker starts jogging on the spot.

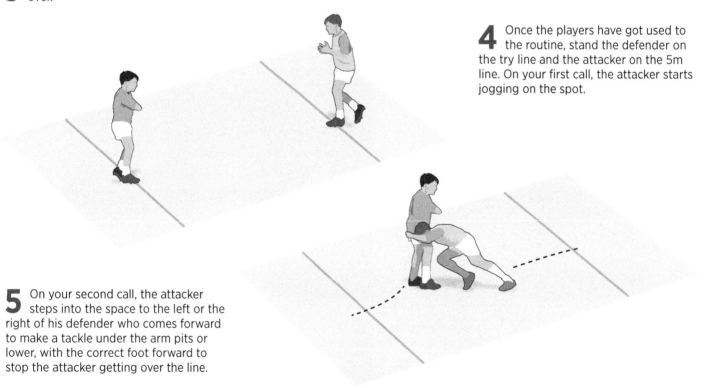

5 On your second call, the attacker steps into the space to the left or the right of his defender who comes forward to make a tackle under the arm pits or lower, with the correct foot forward to stop the attacker getting over the line.

How many players do I need?
Run this activity with as many pairs as you can. Make sure they all have enough space to drive through the tackle.

Key

Ground covered   **Direction of run**

- - - - - - - - →

U11-U12
EVASION

Use swerves and sidesteps to avoid defenders

ACTIVITY: SIDESTEP MIRRORS

EasiCoach
RUGBY SKILLS ACTIVITIES

CALL OUT — "Be light on your feet" • "Accelerate away after the step" • "Keep your head up"

1 Put a 2m square box in the middle of a 10m x 4m area. Position a ball carrier on each corner of the area.

2 When you say "go", two ball carriers run from opposite corners towards the 2m box. They must go through their own side of the box before stepping back out and running towards one of the other corners.

3 Once the first players have completed their run, the other pair repeat the exercise. Get each player to run across 10 times before changing players.

4 Once players are confident running through the box at pace, set up a 10m square area with cones at halfway points on each side. Put an attacker with a ball on one corner and a defender on the opposite corner.

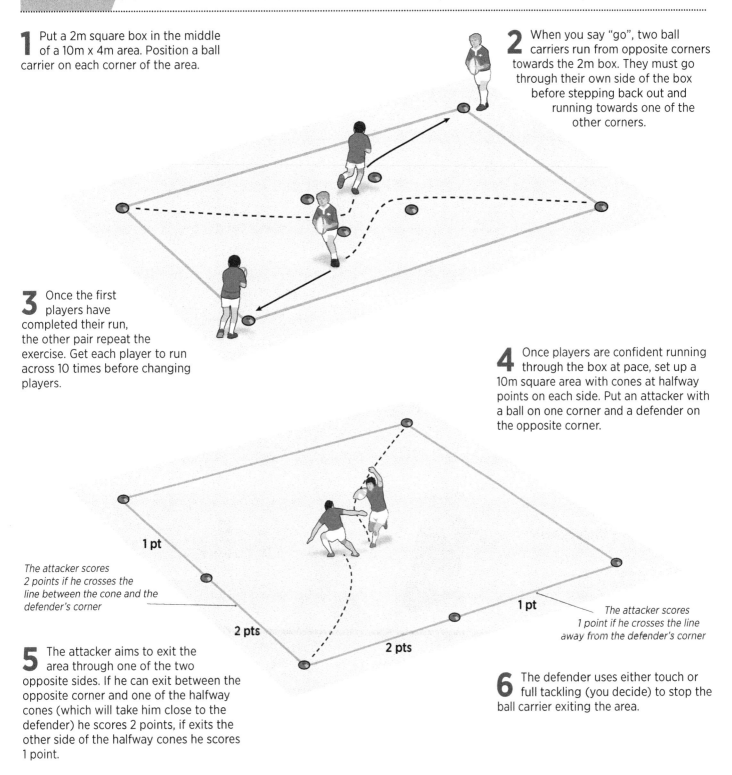

1 pt

The attacker scores 2 points if he crosses the line between the cone and the defender's corner

2 pts

2 pts

1 pt

The attacker scores 1 point if he crosses the line away from the defender's corner

5 The attacker aims to exit the area through one of the two opposite sides. If he can exit between the opposite corner and one of the halfway cones (which will take him close to the defender) he scores 2 points, if exits the other side of the halfway cones he scores 1 point.

6 The defender uses either touch or full tackling (you decide) to stop the ball carrier exiting the area.

How many players do I need?
You need four players for this activity. With more players, set up another area to get them practising their footwork.

Key

Ground covered   **Direction of run**

- - - - - - →

Commit the defender then change direction

ACTIVITY: COMMIT AND BEAT DEFENDERS

CALL OUT "Arc towards the defender" • "As the defender sits to make the tackle, step to one side"

1 Set up a 6m square area with a 3m square box inside it. Position an attacker with a ball on one corner of the 6m area and a defender on an adjacent corner.

2 When you say "go", the players run into the 3m square from opposite sides.

3 The attacker aims to run through the small square, using a sidestep to commit and beat the defender. The defender aims to stop him with a full tackle.

4 When the players start to anticipate what each other is going to do, mix things up by changing starting points so they come into the box from different angles.

5 Finally, play a 3v3 in a 15m x 10m box. A feeder passes the ball into the attacking team before they enter the box, with the defending team starting 5m inside the box. Allow offloads but not rucks. The attacking team aims to get over the defenders' line.

✓ Making a sidestep

Put simply, the sidestep is making a defender think you're going to run one way, but actually going another.

To do this, the attacker runs at the defender and, when he's just in front of him, puts all his weight on one foot to make it look like he's going in that direction. As the defender steps across to cover, the attacker transfers his weight onto his other foot and steps inside, and past, the defender.

How many players do I need?
You need two players to run this activity, but it is very quick so if necessary you can line up lots of players on each corner.

Key

Ground covered   **Direction of run**

– – – – – – – –   ⟶

Change direction with the ball in two hands

ACTIVITY: EVASION TRIANGLES

CALL OUT "Two hands on the ball" • "Keep running forward fast" • "Change direction with conviction"

1 Use three different coloured cones to mark out a 3m triangle. Put a cone 2m either side of the triangle to form gates. Repeat the set up 5m away so that you have two triangles with side gates facing each other. Put a defender inside one triangle and an attacker with a ball just behind the other, facing him.

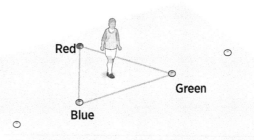

2 When you call out a colour, the attacker runs over that coloured cone in his triangle and then runs through one of the gates either side of the triangle opposite.

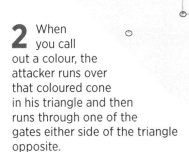

3 In the meantime, the defender touches the coloured cone in his triangle and then reaches out to try to touch the attacker while keeping one foot inside the triangle.

4 Repeat until the players have become confident in changing directions and then make the gates beside the triangle a bit smaller, or make the triangle itself a bit bigger.

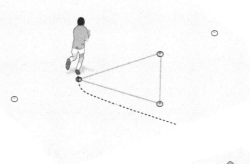

5 Develop by having a supporting player running behind the ball carrier. If the ball carrier is touched, he has two seconds to pass the ball to the supporting player who can run through.

How many players do I need?
You need two players to run this activity, but it is very quick so if necessary you can line up lots of players.

Key
Ground covered
- - - - - - - -

Spin out of contact and pass to support runners

EasiCoach
RUGBY SKILLS ACTIVITIES

ACTIVITY: BUMP AND SPIN TRIANGLES

CALL OUT "Plant your foot close to the middle of the defender and then spin off" • "Keep the ball away from the defender"

1 Mark out a 5m triangle. Put a defender on each corner of the triangle and three attackers and a feeder opposite one corner. The first attacker starts 1m from the defender in front of him.

2 When you say "go", the feeder passes the ball to the first attacker who moves forward and spins away from the defender. The defender tries to grab and hold the attacker.

Let the players work out their own way to spin out of a tackle. However, it does start with the ball carrier planting one foot near the tackler and then spinning away so that the ball is out of reach of the tackler

3 If the attacker succeeds in beating the defender, he then attacks the next defender on the side he has spun out to, using the attackers on his inside and outside to pass to.

4 Develop by allowing the third defender to move across to support the second defender. The ball carrier can pass, offload in contact or go to ground and be supported.

How many players do I need?
You need seven players for this activity. If you have more, set up other triangles – remember to allow plenty of space between them.

Key

Ground covered	Pass	Direction of run
– – – – – – –	· · · · · · ·▶	———▶

© **EasiCoach Rugby Skills Activities**

U11-U12
HANDLING

Pass to a target and run on to a pass at pace

ACTIVITY: CATCH AND PASS

CALL OUT "Keep your hands out and chest high" • "Receive the ball early" • "Look at the receiver as you pass" • "Transfer your hands across the chest and pass"

1 Set out a 5m square area. Put player 1 in the middle on the left side, player 2 in the middle on the start line and player 3 in the middle on the right side.

2 Stage 1 (walking) – Give player 1 a ball. When you say "go", he passes the ball to player 2 who catches and walks about three-quarters of the way across the area before passing back to player 3.

3 Player 2 walks to the end of the area, turns, gets a pass from player 3, walks on and passes to player 1.

4 Increase the speed the player in the middle moves, receives and passes. When proficient, increase the length of the pass by making the area bigger, then add another passer to make two players in the middle.

5 Stage 2 – Introduce a defender who will provide pressure by moving forward from challenge player 2. Again, player 1 passes to player 2 who catches and passes to player 3 under pressure from the defender. Start at walking pace and develop into a run to increase the intensity of the skill.

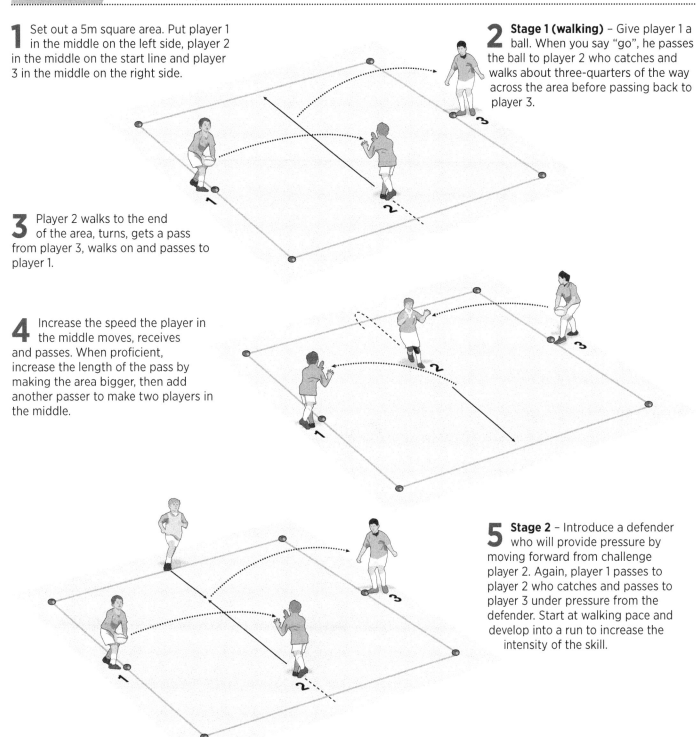

How many players do I need?
You need three players for stage 1 and a fourth for stage 2. With more players set out more 5m squares.

Key
Ground covered	Pass	Direction of run
- - - - - - -	· · · · · · ▸	──────▸

Take and give a pass under pressure and at pace

ACTIVITY: CREATING AN OVERLAP

> **CALL OUT** — "Keep the ball away from the body"

1 Set up a 15m x 9m area. Split the area into three 3m channels and number the channels 1, 2 and 3.

2 Play 3v2 – put attackers in all three channels starting at one end of the area and defenders in channels 1 and 2 only, starting at the opposite end. Put a feeder to the side of channel 1.

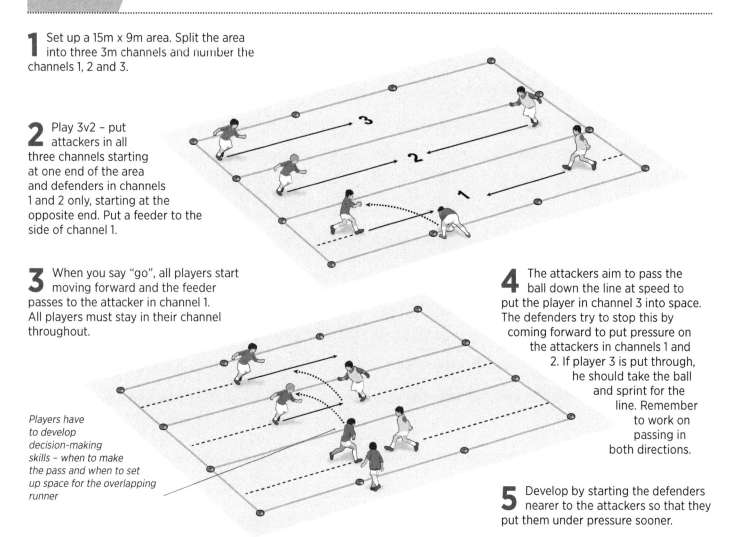

3 When you say "go", all players start moving forward and the feeder passes to the attacker in channel 1. All players must stay in their channel throughout.

Players have to develop decision-making skills – when to make the pass and when to set up space for the overlapping runner

4 The attackers aim to pass the ball down the line at speed to put the player in channel 3 into space. The defenders try to stop this by coming forward to put pressure on the attackers in channels 1 and 2. If player 3 is put through, he should take the ball and sprint for the line. Remember to work on passing in both directions.

5 Develop by starting the defenders nearer to the attackers so that they put them under pressure sooner.

✓ Catching and passing at pace

Catch the ball away from the body

Keep the ball away from the body between catching and passing – do not clutch it to the chest

Pass accurately with hands following through to the target

How many players do I need?

Start with 3v2, but you could add more channels and play up to 5v4, or line up players ready to come on.

Key

Ground covered	Pass	Direction of run
- - - - - - -	·······▶	───▶

Fix a defender and pass in front of support player

ACTIVITY: PASSING UNDER PRESSURE

CALL OUT "Reach for the ball to take it early" • "Try and run at match pace" • "Look where you're passing"

1 Put two attackers, 2m apart, on one side of the 6m x 4m area. Position a ruck pad holder on the other side of the area 4m from the first attacker. Position a feeder to the side of the area 2m from the first attacker.

2 When you say "go", the first attacker accelerates directly at the ruck pad holder, who also advances at pace.

3 As the players advance, the ball is fed to the attacker about 1m from the ruck pad holder and, just before contact, he passes the ball to the second attacker who is running in support.

4 Repeat from both ends of the area, making sure every player tries out every role.

5 Develop by varying the length of pass the first attacker has to make – short or long.

6 When mastered, play a 3v2 so the first and second receivers are under intense pressure from the pad holders and have to move the ball quickly to the third attacker. Or, the ruck pad holders can move onto the next defender. The ball carrier can dummy pass and go himself.

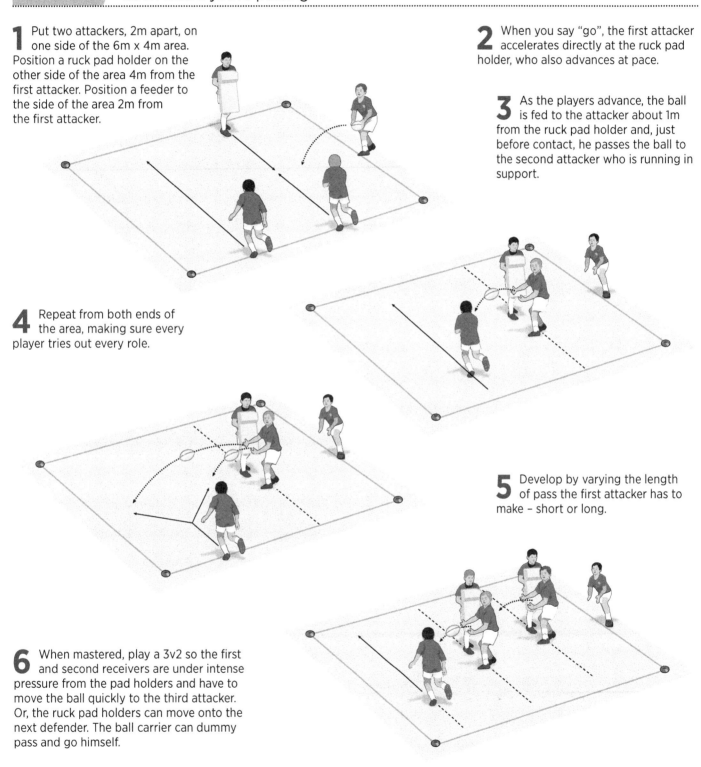

How many players do I need?
You need four players for the first part of the activity and two more for the development.

Key

Ground covered	Pass	Direction of run
– – – – – – –	·················▶	⟶

Spin a long miss pass

ACTIVITY: SPINNING A MISS PASS

CALL OUT   "Roll the ball out of the hand" • "Finish the pass with the palm up and the ball touching your little finger last"

1 Start by putting your players into pairs and getting them practising their spin passes. To do this, they put one hand on the ball, put the ball on the hip and then pass the ball 5m to a partner. First they do this with either hand. Then they do it with both hands on the ball.

✓ **Making a spin pass**

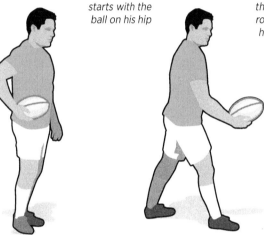

The ball carrier starts with the ball on his hip

He steps towards the catcher and rolls the ball off his hand to the catcher

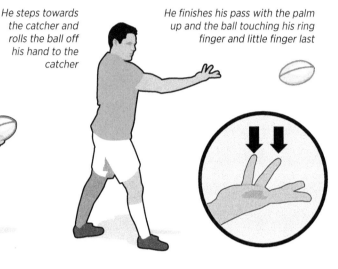

He finishes his pass with the palm up and the ball touching his ring finger and little finger last

2 When the players are comfortable spinning the ball off either hand, move on to the activity.

3 Set out a 20m square area. Put three receivers on one side with 5m between them. Put three cones in the middle of the area – one in front of each receiver. Place a feeder on the right side of the area, about 5m along.

4 When you say "go", all receivers run forward. The feeder passes to the first receiver who runs on to the cone in front of him and throws a hard, spinning miss pass in front of the second receiver to the third receiver (the miss pass is so called because it misses out one or more players in the line).

5 The third receiver has to make a decision to go either left or right of the cone, so he has to ensure he hits the ball at full pace and at an angle that will take him to the side of the cone he has chosen. He should then sprint to the far side of the area.

How many players do I need?
You need four players for the activity. Put players into pairs and get them practising spin passing while they wait their turn.

Key

Ground covered	Pass	Direction of run
– – – – –	·······▶	———▶

Change angles and make a switch pass

ACTIVITY: THE SWITCH PASS

> **CALL OUT** "Engage on the catch, take the ball forward then cut across" • "Leave the ball on the hip, don't pass it"

1 Stand two players 7m apart and place a gate of tackle tubes or cones 7m in front of the second player. Put a feeder to the side, about 5m from the first player

2 When you say "go", the first player runs forward to take a pass from the feeder then cuts diagonally across the area towards the tackle tubes. At the same time, the second player makes a run that crosses just behind the run of the first player.

Hold the ball in two hands so that one end is pointing to the floor. Move the ball round the hip and use the wrists to flip it up and into the path of the runner

3 As the players are about to cross, the first player passes the ball off his hip into the path of the second player. The first player then runs through the gate in the tubes, so he finishes facing up the pitch and the second player runs to the side of the tubes.

4 Develop this by putting in one or two defenders who run from behind the tackle tubes to put pressure on the passer and receiver.

How many players do I need?
You need three players to start with and another for the development. Line players up so that they can run through the activity quickly.

Key

Ground covered	Pass	Direction of run
– – – – – –	· · · · · · · ▸	⟶

Create an extra player in attack

ACTIVITY: MAKING THE EXTRA MAN

> **CALL OUT** "Run straight before you pass, then loop behind" • "Turn the shoulders to pass" • "Call for the ball"

1 Set up a line of three cones – the second cone 3m in front of the first and the third 5m in front of the second and slightly offset to the left. Repeat with two more identical lines 3m apart to form two channels.

2 Place an attacker at the start of each channel. Put a feeder to the right of the first receiver.

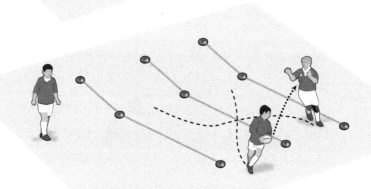

3 When you say "go", the two attackers run forward through their channels and the feeder passes the ball to the first attacker.

4 Once the first attacker has reached the second cone, he passes the ball to the second attacker.

5 The second attacker then angles his run inside to the first channel and then passes at the end of that channel to the first attacker who has run outside him into the second channel.

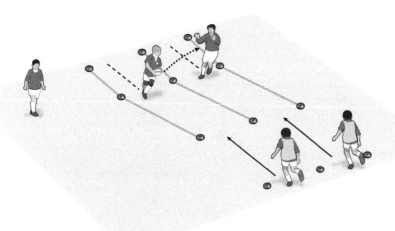

6 Develop by putting two defenders 5m away from the ends of the channels. They walk/run forward to pressurise the attackers as they advance through the channels.

How many players do I need?
You need three players to start with and two more for the development. Line players up to run through the channels.

Key

Ground covered	Pass	Direction of run
– – – – – – –	·······▶	⟶

© **EasiCoach Rugby Skills Activities**

Make an offload pass after a tackle

ACTIVITY: KEEP THE BALL ALIVE

CALL OUT "Aim to get beyond the tackler before passing" • "Keep two hands on the ball" • "In support, run behind the ball carrier and call for the ball"

1 Mark out a 10m x 4m area. Put two defenders on one knee at 3m and 7m into the area and three attackers at the far end of the area facing them. Give a ball to one of the attackers.

2 When you say "go", the three attackers run forward. The first attacker runs at the first defender and then steps to one side to take a tackle.

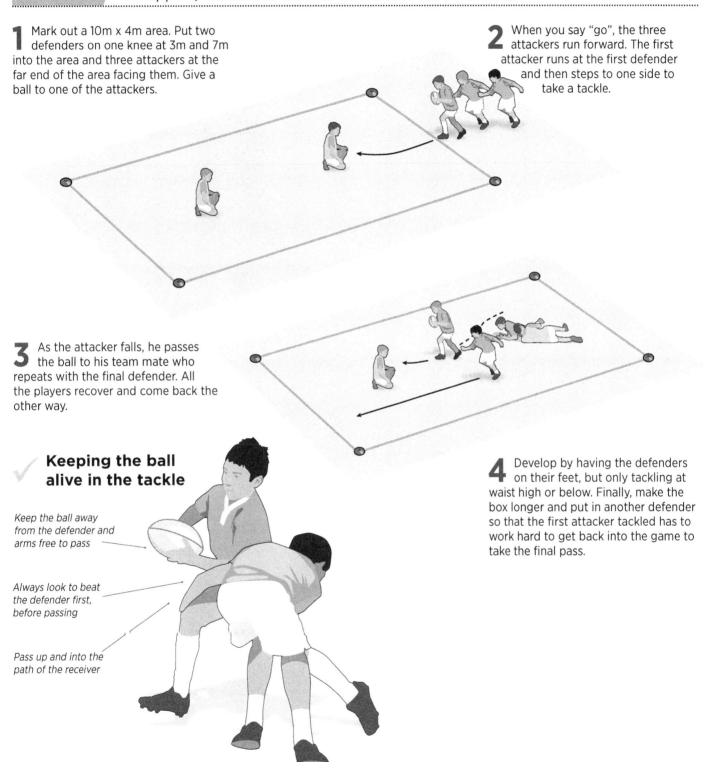

3 As the attacker falls, he passes the ball to his team mate who repeats with the final defender. All the players recover and come back the other way.

4 Develop by having the defenders on their feet, but only tackling at waist high or below. Finally, make the box longer and put in another defender so that the first attacker tackled has to work hard to get back into the game to take the final pass.

✓ **Keeping the ball alive in the tackle**

Keep the ball away from the defender and arms free to pass

Always look to beat the defender first, before passing

Pass up and into the path of the receiver

How many players do I need?
Run this activity with five players. With more players, set up a couple of areas side by side.

Key

Ground covered	Direction of run
– – – – – –	—→

Pass off the floor
ACTIVITY: THE CLEARANCE PASS

CALL OUT "Always arrive square" • "Chest over the ball, ball near back foot"

✓ Getting in position for a clearance pass

Ball too close to the back foot makes it a laboured pass and risks being interfered with

Ball too close to the front foot makes it hard to generate power

Ball positioned between the middle and the back foot with the chest over the ball allows a low sweep of the arms. Follow through to the receiver

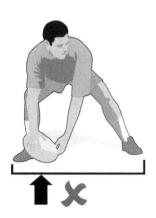  

The front foot should be pointing towards the receiver

1 Start by getting players used to the correct set-up of a clearance pass (above), with the correct ball and foot placement, a low body position and hands following through to the receiver.

The pole indicates where a second defender would stand

2 Next, set out a tackle tube with a pole 3m to one side and a receiver 15m back from the pole. Place two coloured cones about 10m in front of you and 15m apart You kneel behind the tackle tube with balls next to you.

Blue

Green

3 Call a player towards you from one of the cones. Place a ball on the ground on his side of the tube and call a type of pass that you want him to perform: either "Clearance", "Pull back" or "Scoot".

4 Work on both hands, focusing on the passer arriving square, with the shoulders and hips facing up the pitch. Get the player coming to the side of the tube from both cones so that he changes his angle of approach.

"Clearance" **"Pull back"** **"Scoot"**

The player sweeps the ball away immediately

The player steps back from the tackle tube before delivering the pass (you can try to swipe the ball)

The player picks up, runs out and squares up on the pole before passing to the receiver

How many players do I need?
You need three players in this activity. Line up players to come in and make the pass and have players outside the receiver to take passes.

Key
Ground covered — — — — | Pass ••••••••▶ | Direction of run ——▶

© EasiCoach Rugby Skills Activities

U11-U12

KICKING

Kick accurately to a target

ACTIVITY: KICK TO A TARGET

CALL OUT "The ball is held correctly with the toe pointed when punting" • "Don't throw the ball up to kick - drop it"

1 Set out two 2m cone gates 15m apart. Put two players behind each gate and give one of the players a ball. When you say "go", the ball holder passes to the player next to him.

2 The second player catches the ball then aims to kick it into the opposite "kicking zone", which is through the opposite gate (the ball should land no more than 5m behind the gate).

3 One of the players opposite catches the ball and then passes it to his partner to kick back. Players take turns passing, kicking and catching.

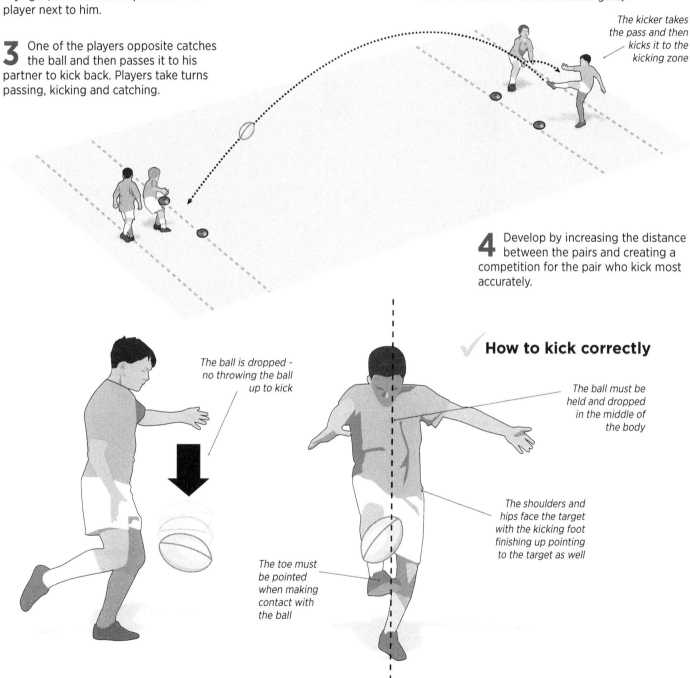

The kicker takes the pass and then kicks it to the kicking zone

4 Develop by increasing the distance between the pairs and creating a competition for the pair who kick most accurately.

The ball is dropped - no throwing the ball up to kick

✓ How to kick correctly

The ball must be held and dropped in the middle of the body

The shoulders and hips face the target with the kicking foot finishing up pointing to the target as well

The toe must be pointed when making contact with the ball

How many players do I need?

You need four players for this activity. If you have space, set out more cone gates and get as many players as possible kicking to each other.

Key
Pass/Kick
· · · · · · · · · · ▶

Make a cradle when catching a high ball

ACTIVITY: CATCHING THE HIGH BALL

CALL OUT "Make your arms like a cradle to gather the ball" • "Get your body into a "T" shape so that the ball spills backwards, not forwards"

✓ Catching a high ball

Run forward, watching the flight of the ball

Form a cradle with the arms – this encourages safe pouching of the ball

If the player is skilful enough, he can jump up, while making the "T" shape

Land with a solid base with the ball gripped firmly, one foot in front of the other, ready to move forward

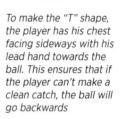

Direction of play

To make the "T" shape, the player has his chest facing sideways with his lead hand towards the ball. This ensures that if the player can't make a clean catch, the ball will go backwards

1 Divide players into groups of three and give each group a ball. Tell each group to get into a 15m triangle and kick the ball high to each other in rotation.

2 Once players are comfortable kicking and catching, extend the distance and height of kick to 25m: One player kicks, one chases and one receives. The chaser causes a distraction but no contact is to be made.

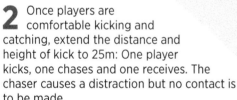

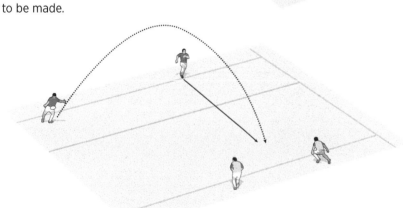

3 Finally play 2v2, expand the distance for the aerial kick with kickers on the halfway line and receivers behind the 22m line. The receiver is defined by where the kick is directed to and the chaser is encouraged to challenge for the ball. The two receivers must communicate who is challenging to receive and who is supporting.

How many players do I need?
You need three players to start with and a fourth for the 2v2 game. Get as many groups of three kicking as space will allow.

Key

Ground covered	Pass/Kick	Direction of run
– – – – –	·······▶	───▶

U13-U16
CONTACT

Change body position to improve ball placement

ACTIVITY: PROTECT THE BALL

CALL OUT "Step hard round the feeder" • "Drop to the ground and get into position quickly"

1 Set out two cones, 8m apart. Put a feeder 5m back from the first cone with a pile of balls at his feet. Line your players up by the first cone.

2 When you say "go", the first player comes forward and takes a pass from the feeder. You then shout out a ball placement shape – "jack knife", "long" or "power roll".

3 The player takes the pass, steps past the feeder and then goes to ground behind the rear cone to perform the required placement shape.

4 As soon as he is past the feeder, the next player comes forward and repeats, stepping to the other side.

5 Develop by having the previous placement player act as a tackler. In this case, work at 50% intensity so the players concentrate on good technique.

✓ **Perfecting placement shapes**

"Jack knife"   **"Long"**

Feet and ball towards the try line   *Ball to own try line, feet to theirs*

"Power roll"

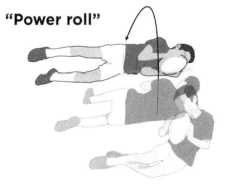

Roll backwards twice before ball placement

How many players do I need?
You can line up as many players as you like, as long as you have enough balls.

Key

Ground covered	Pass	Direction of run
– – – – –	· · · · · · · ▶	───────▶

Fend off defenders with good ball transfer

ACTIVITY: THE POWER STEP

CALL OUT "Keep the ball away from the defender" • "Push with a bent arm" • "Drive forward"

1 Mark out a 2m triangle of cones and put a tackle tube behind it. Put a feeder to one side of the triangle and an attacker by a starting cone about 6m in front of the triangle.

2 When you say "go", the attacker runs forward, takes a pass from the feeder and runs into the triangle. He then steps out to one side of the triangle and forward, and uses a hand to fend off the tube at the same time.

3 When players have mastered fending off the tackle tube, mark out a 5m line and position ruck pad holders at 2m and 4m along the line, one standing just to the left and the other to the right. Put attackers at either end of the line and give the first attacker a ball.

4 When you say "go", the first attacker runs forward, fends off the first ruck pad holder with one hand, then transfers the ball to the other hand and fends off the second ruck pad holder. At the end of the line he passes to the next attacker who repeats, going back the other way.

✓ **Fending off a defender**

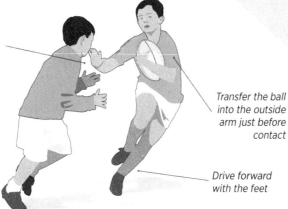

Use a bent arm to push the flat palm of the hand into the chest or shoulder of the defender

Transfer the ball into the outside arm just before contact

Drive forward with the feet

How many players do I need?
You need two players for the first part of the activity and five for the second part.

Key

Ground covered	Pass	Direction of run
- - - - - - -	................▶	———————▶

Create a driving maul from a lineout

ACTIVITY: CATCH AND DRIVE

> **CALL OUT** "Bind in front of the jumper" • "Keep your feet in line and drive forward" • "Get round the maul quickly to rip the ball"

1 Start with a pod of three players – one player (the catcher) has the ball and the supporters bind on making sure they have their feet, shoulders, hips and arms in the right places (see diagram, right).

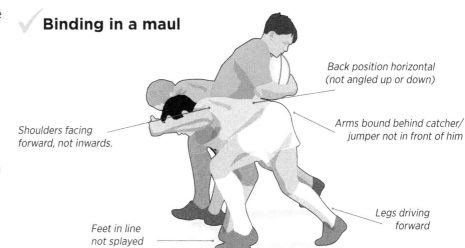

✓ **Binding in a maul**

Back position horizontal (not angled up or down)

Arms bound behind catcher/ jumper not in front of him

Shoulders facing forward, not inwards.

Legs driving forward

Feet in line not splayed

2 Once players are comfortable getting into the correct positions, add a fourth player to the pod plus a thrower, then set out three different coloured cones along the touchline at 10m intervals. Put a ball next to each cone.

3 When you call out a colour, here "Red", the players run to that cone and line up for a line out, with the lifters/ support players (S) either side of the jumper/catcher (J) and 4 at the back acting as the ripper.

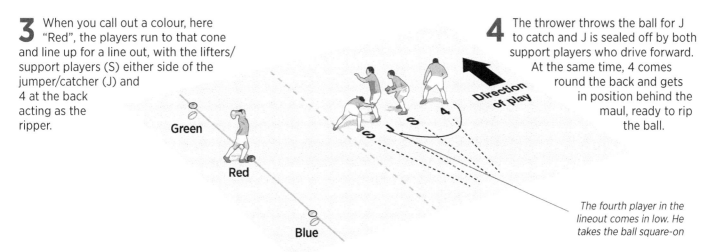

Green

Red

Blue

4 The thrower throws the ball for J to catch and J is sealed off by both support players who drive forward. At the same time, 4 comes round the back and gets in position behind the maul, ready to rip the ball.

Direction of play

The fourth player in the lineout comes in low. He takes the ball square-on

5 Progress to a full lineout with two more players (5 and 6) binding on to 4 once he has the ball.

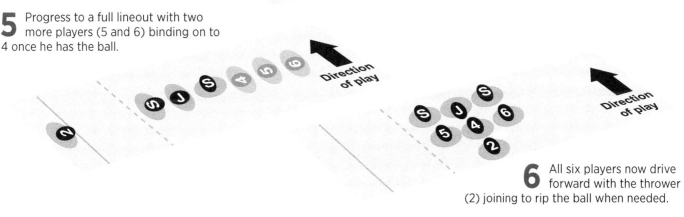

Direction of play

Direction of play

6 All six players now drive forward with the thrower (2) joining to rip the ball when needed.

How many players do I need?
Start with three players and build to seven. With more players, run several lineout pods simultaneously.

Key

Ground covered	Direction of run
- - - - - - - -	⟶

Decide how many players are needed in an attack

ACTIVITY: ATTACK WHAT YOU SEE

CALL OUT "Use passing and offloads if there are low numbers of defenders." • "In contact, look to clear out the threats"

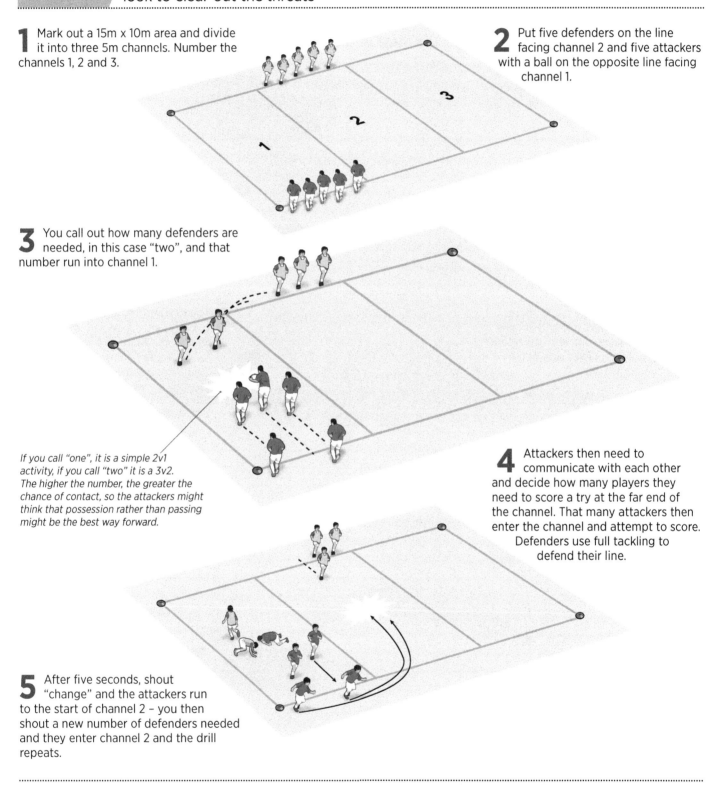

1 Mark out a 15m x 10m area and divide it into three 5m channels. Number the channels 1, 2 and 3.

2 Put five defenders on the line facing channel 2 and five attackers with a ball on the opposite line facing channel 1.

3 You call out how many defenders are needed, in this case "two", and that number run into channel 1.

If you call "one", it is a simple 2v1 activity, if you call "two" it is a 3v2. The higher the number, the greater the chance of contact, so the attackers might think that possession rather than passing might be the best way forward.

4 Attackers then need to communicate with each other and decide how many players they need to score a try at the far end of the channel. That many attackers then enter the channel and attempt to score. Defenders use full tackling to defend their line.

5 After five seconds, shout "change" and the attackers run to the start of channel 2 – you then shout a new number of defenders needed and they enter channel 2 and the drill repeats.

How many players do I need?
You need 10 players for this activity. If you have more, set up another 15m x 10m area and run another game alongside.

Key
Ground covered   **Direction of run**
- - - - - - - -   →

Clear the ruck and drive over the ball

ACTIVITY: TARGET THE BALL AT A RUCK

CALL OUT — "Drive into the contact area" • "Stay low in contact" • "Protect the ball"

1 Place three cones 4m apart. Put a ruck pad holder and a defender 2m behind and 2m to the side of each cone.

2 Put four attackers with a ball on the first cone. Their aim is to clear the three rucks accurately and ensure they protect and drive beyond the ball.

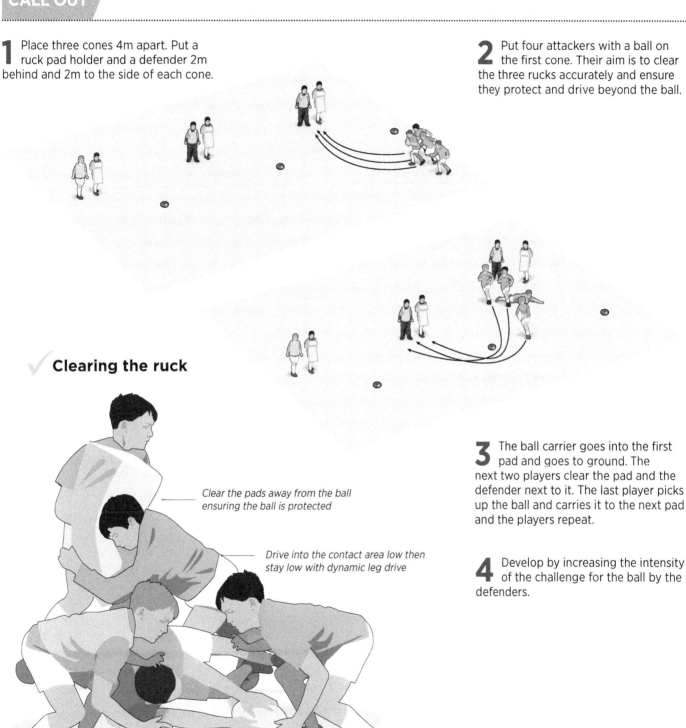

✓ **Clearing the ruck**

Clear the pads away from the ball ensuring the ball is protected

Drive into the contact area low then stay low with dynamic leg drive

Always focus on the ball

3 The ball carrier goes into the first pad and goes to ground. The next two players clear the pad and the defender next to it. The last player picks up the ball and carries it to the next pad and the players repeat.

4 Develop by increasing the intensity of the challenge for the ball by the defenders.

How many players do I need?
You need 10 players for this activity. If you have more, line up groups of four attackers ready to come on. Rotate the defenders regularly.

Key
Direction of run
⟶

Choose the right option in contact

ACTIVITY: DIFFERENT OPTIONS AT CONTACT

CALL OUT "Aim to get to the sides of the tackler" • "Call early to help ball carrier" • "Get the shoulder into the ball to rip"

1 Mark out a 12m square area then divide it into two boxes – box A is 4m wide and box B is 8m wide. Have four attackers, one with a ball, stand at one end of the line that divides the two boxes. Place defenders at 4m and 8m on the dividing line.

2 Shout a box to attack, here "B", and the ball carrier runs into the box followed by the other attackers. At the same time, the first defender comes forward.

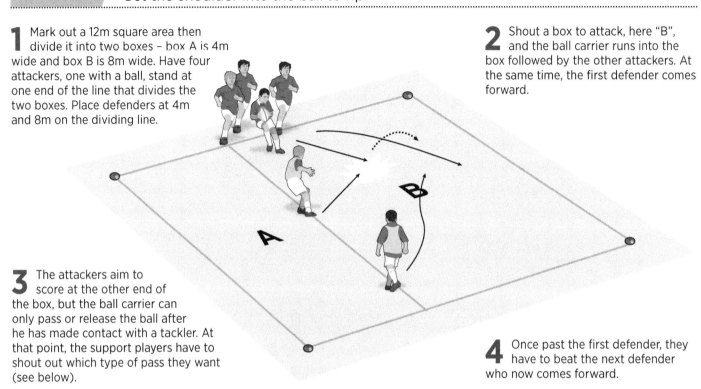

3 The attackers aim to score at the other end of the box, but the ball carrier can only pass or release the ball after he has made contact with a tackler. At that point, the support players have to shout out which type of pass they want (see below).

4 Once past the first defender, they have to beat the next defender who now comes forward.

✓ Ripping the ball

Rip the ball from the ball carrier by getting close, wrapping arms around the ball and ripping it down and away with the shoulders.

If the ball carrier and ripper are too far away, the ball can get dislodged or dropped.

✓ Popping the ball up

The ball carrier "pops" the ball up from the ground, pushing the ball at his team mate like a netball pass.

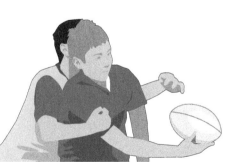

✓ Offloading the ball

Turn the shoulders, keeping the hand under the ball to hook it to the support player and away from the defender

How many players do I need?

You need six players for this activity. If you have more, set up another area and run another game alongside.

Key

Pass ·····▶

Direction of run ──▶

© **EasiCoach Rugby Skills Activities**

Lean into contact and drive through

ACTIVITY: LEAN INTO CONTACT

CALL OUT   "Take short steps" • "Accelerate quickly into contact" • "Keep low into contact"

1 Mark out a 5m square area. Put two ruck pad holders at the end of the area about arm's distance apart.

2 Have a ball carrier start at the opposite end of the area and run first at one ruck pad holder and then drive through the gap between the two. He aims to smash through and out the other side.

3 Have the ruck pad holders start further into the box so the ball carrier has to accelerate quicker, as if he is taking a late pass near to the gain line.

Leaning into contact

Take short steps into contact, lean forward, keeping the ball tight to the body and accelerate into contact. Drive through with the legs.

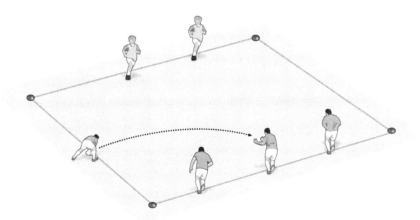

4 Develop by putting three attackers in a 8m x 6m area, being fed by another player. Facing them are two defenders. The ball is passed directly to the middle player who aims to break through the defenders. If he can't, he can offload or go to ground. The support players can take an offload or drive the player through contact or win the ruck.

How many players do I need?
You need three players for the first part of the activity and six for the development.

Key

Pass
................▶

Direction of run
——————▶

Call the best options in contact for the ball carrier

EasiCoach
RUGBY SKILLS ACTIVITIES

ACTIVITY: SUPPORT THE BALL CARRIER IN CONTACT

CALL OUT — "Swoop early to pick up the ball" • "Hands up to receive a pop pass" • "Get the shoulder into the ball to rip and drive"

1 Mark out three 5m x 2m boxes each 1m from the next and staggered by 3m. Put a ruck pad holder in each box and a pair of players with a ball about 2m in front of the ruck pad holders.

2 Starting with "Pick", the ball carrier goes into the ruck pad, goes to ground, the supporting player shouts "My pick" and swoops down to pick up the ball (see below). The players recover and move to the next ruck pad.

3 At the next ruck pad, the ball carrier steps into the ruck pad and pops the ball to his team mate as he bounces off. The support player shouts "My pop".

4 At the last pad, the ball carrier steps into the ruck pad, turns and the support player shouts "My rip" and drives himself into the ball carrier and rips down and away with the ball.

5 The players cycle through each one. You can have the players working on the same skill at all three, or mix up the skills.

6 Develop by taking away the ruck pads, and also by working in threes. The players cycle through each one. You can have the players working on the same skill at all three, or mix up the skills.

"My pick"

Swoop down and put the front foot next to the ball to pick and go.

"My pop"

Put hands up to receive the ball. The pass should be popped into the air in front of the receiver.

"My rip"

Drive into the ball carrier before ripping the ball.

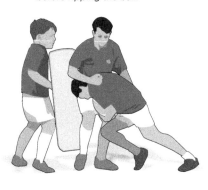

How many players do I need?
Start with nine players, but you can line up lots of pairs to run through the boxes, or set up more boxes alongside.

Key

Ground covered — — — — — — —

Direction of run ⟶

U13-U16
DEFENCE

Make tackles from different starting positions

ACTIVITY: WORK ON TACKLE TECHNIQUE

EasiCoach
RUGBY SKILLS ACTIVITIES

CALL OUT "Get close to ball carrier" • "Get your head to the side of ball carrier, not in front" • "Drive with your legs to finish the tackle"

1 Divide your players into pairs, an attacker with a ball and a defender, and put each pair in a 5m square area.

2 Play a series of 1v1s inside the square, each time from a different starting position: Standing 1m apart facing each other, standing 1m apart with backs to each other, sitting back to back, or facing each other 1m apart in press up position.

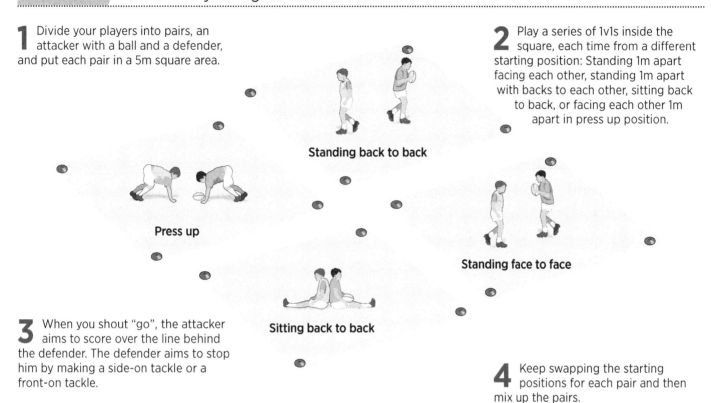

Standing back to back

Press up

Standing face to face

Sitting back to back

3 When you shout "go", the attacker aims to score over the line behind the defender. The defender aims to stop him by making a side-on tackle or a front-on tackle.

4 Keep swapping the starting positions for each pair and then mix up the pairs.

✓ Making a side-on tackle

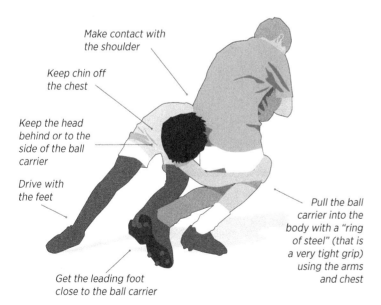

Make contact with the shoulder

Keep chin off the chest

Keep the head behind or to the side of the ball carrier

Drive with the feet

Get the leading foot close to the ball carrier

Pull the ball carrier into the body with a "ring of steel" (that is a very tight grip) using the arms and chest

✓ Making a front-on tackle

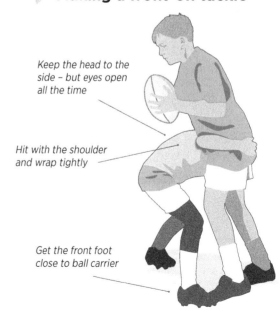

Keep the head to the side – but eyes open all the time

Hit with the shoulder and wrap tightly

Get the front foot close to ball carrier

How many players do I need?
As many pairs as you have balls and space for.

Key

Use footwork to get close to the ball carrier

ACTIVITY: FRONT-ON TACKLING

> **CALL OUT** "Use shuffling steps like a boxer" • "Crouch low and hit with the shoulder" • "Drive through the ruck pad"

1 Start by getting a defender to slowly approach a ball carrier using small, shuffling "boxing" steps then crouch to get under the ball, lift the attacker shoulder high and place him down safely after carrying him 2m.

2 Once players have mastered this shuffling approach and crouch, begin the activity in the different boxes.

3 Set out three boxes – 7m x 3m, 7m x 5m and 7m x 10m – and put a ruck pad holder at the end of each. Put a tackler at the start of the first box, opposite the ruck pad holder.

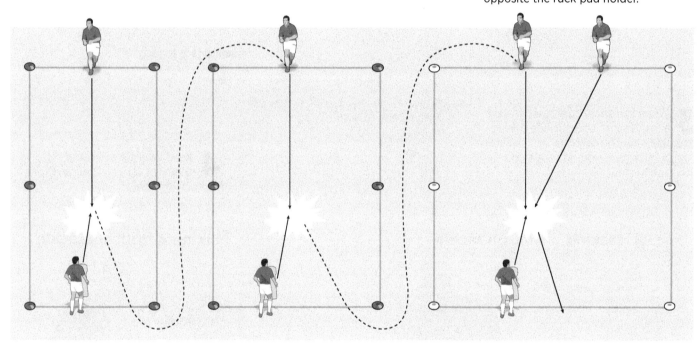

4 When you say "go", the tackler runs into the box and the ruck pad holder moves forward. The tackler drives in low to the ruck pad holder who drops the pad. The tackler goes to ground, holding the pad, then releases it, gets to his feet and runs into the next box where he repeats the tackle. In the widest box, he is joined by another tackler and they both take out the ruck pad holder – one tackling high, the other low.

Use foot movement like a boxer, getting in close and crouching as if ready to deliver a punch. This means the tackler makes contact on his terms – front-on and at pace.

By grabbing the pad after contact, tacklers get into the habit of bringing players to ground.

How many players do I need?
Put players into pairs to practise the lifting technique. You will need five players for the second part of the activity.

Key

Ground covered	Pass	Direction of run
– – – – –	·······▶	───▶

Tackle front-on and with power

ACTIVITY: EXPLOSIVE TACKLING

CALL OUT "Stay balanced" • "Dip low and drive up" • "Get your arms around pad and player"

✓ **Moving into a tackle**

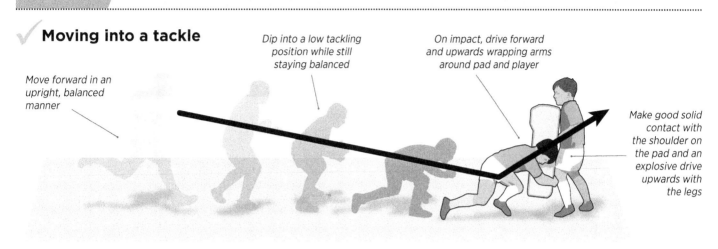

Move forward in an upright, balanced manner

Dip into a low tackling position while still staying balanced

On impact, drive forward and upwards wrapping arms around pad and player

Make good solid contact with the shoulder on the pad and an explosive drive upwards with the legs

1 Set out a 15m square area. Have three attackers holding ruck pads on one side, facing three defenders on the opposite side.

2 When you say "go", the ruck pad holders walk forward, while the defenders jog forward. The defenders make a solid front-on tackle, going from low to high into the ruck pad holders.

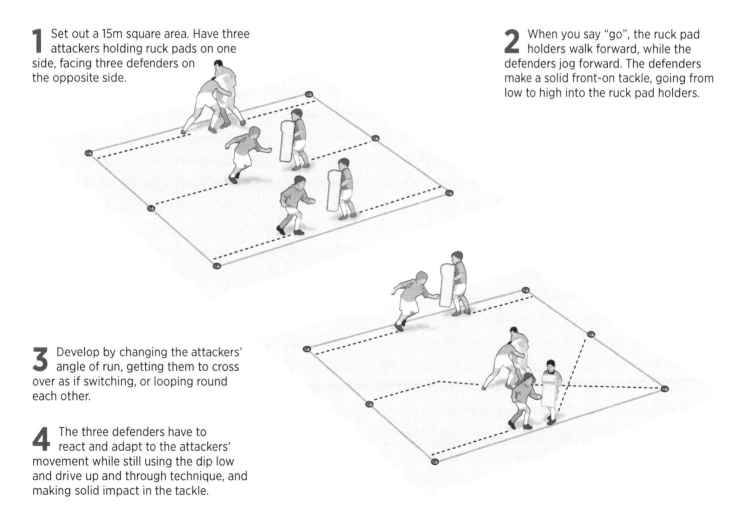

3 Develop by changing the attackers' angle of run, getting them to cross over as if switching, or looping round each other.

4 The three defenders have to react and adapt to the attackers' movement while still using the dip low and drive up and through technique, and making solid impact in the tackle.

How many players do I need?
You need six players. If you have more, rotate defenders and attackers frequently, or set up another area if you have enough pads.

Key
Ground covered
- - - - - - - -

Get in position to make a semi-front-on tackle

ACTIVITY: REACTION TACKLES

> **CALL OUT** "Take short steps to get into position" • "Grip the ball carrier tightly" • "Drive him to the ground"

1 Put a ruck pad holder by a cone. Put a tackler one step in front of him and a ball carrier about 1m behind him. Place a second cone 4m to the left of the first.

2 When you say "go", the tackler two-hand pushes the ruck pad holder. At the same time, the ball carrier runs left.

3 The tackler aims to tackle the ball carrier. The ball carrier can go no wider than the 4m cone.

4 When the tackle is made, new tacklers and ball carriers can come in and take their place. Once players are used to tackling to the left, move the cone to the right of the ruck pad holder.

Take short, quick steps into the ball carrier

Head behind the body or backside of the ball carrier

Grip tightly with the arms and drive the legs to finish the tackle

5 Develop by having two tacklers working together, with the second tackler targeting the ball or aiming to steal it once the tackle is made.

How many players do I need?
As long as you have enough ruck pads, you can get as many threes tackling as you possible.

Key
Ground covered   Direction of run
- - - - - - - →

© **EasiCoach Rugby Skills Activities**

Tackle in pairs

ACTIVITY: DOUBLE TACKLING

CALL OUT "Stay on your feet – don't dive in" • "Second tackler, watch the first tackler and adjust to his actions"

1 Place two tackle tubes, numbered 1 and 2, 5m apart on a line (such as the try line or touchline). Put a line of four players 5m behind each tube.

2 When you call a number, the players at the front of each line run out and tackle that tube.

3 Due to the distance between the tubes, one player will always arrive first. The first arriving tackler must decide whether he's going to stop offloads (tackle high) or stop progress (chop the player down low). The next arriving tackler will adjust to what the first tackler does.

4 Once everyone has had a turn, move the tubes closer together and insist on both players making the tackle at the same time.

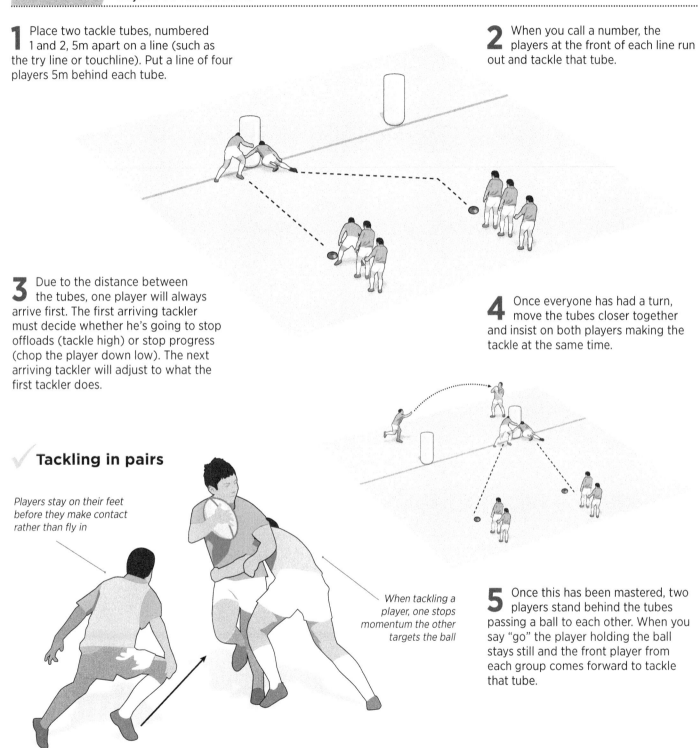

✓ **Tackling in pairs**

Players stay on their feet before they make contact rather than fly in

When tackling a player, one stops momentum the other targets the ball

5 Once this has been mastered, two players stand behind the tubes passing a ball to each other. When you say "go" the player holding the ball stays still and the front player from each group comes forward to tackle that tube.

How many players do I need?
You need eight players for this activity. If you have more, set up more tackle tubes and get more players tackling.

Key

Ground covered	Pass	Direction of run
– – – – – – –	·············▶	———▶

Organise defenders around the ruck

ACTIVITY: DEFENDING AT RUCKS

CALL OUT "Make sure the end defender is opposite the far attacker" • "Come forward together as the ball is passed"

1 Mark out a 20m square area and put a 2m square box at one side to simulate a ruck. Put a ball next to the ruck on one side with a player (usually this will be your number 9) ready to pass to a player outside him (10) who has three support attackers outside him.

2 Four defenders lie on their front behind the ruck just outside the area. When you call "go", they get up, round the ruck and line up opposite the attackers ready to defend.

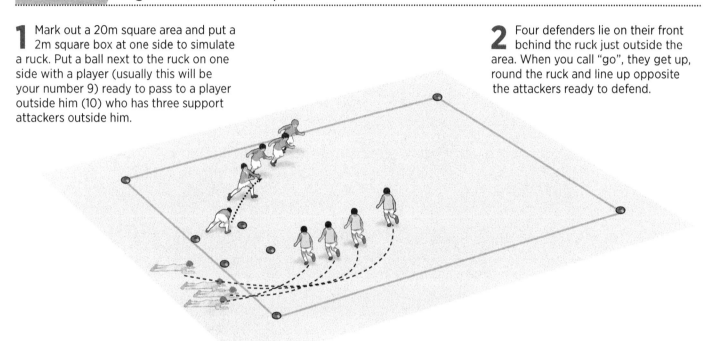

3 As the defenders organise themselves, the 9 passes to the 10 and the attack comes forward while the defenders have to manage their channel. The 9 can run himself if there is a gap.

4 Defenders use touch tackling but the tackles must be on the front of the ball carrier to count.

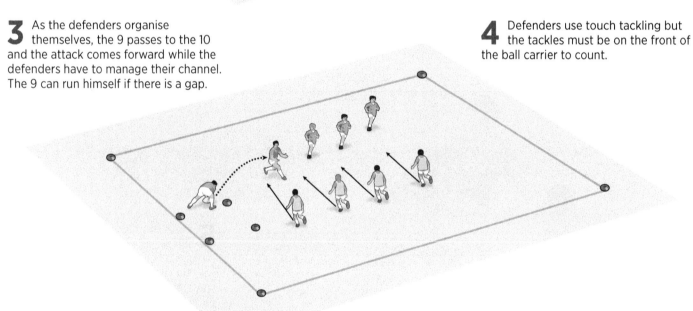

5 Experiment with the attackers aligning spread out or close together to see how the defence reacts.

How many players do I need?

You need nine players to run this activity. If you have more, set up another playing area and run another game alongside.

Key

Ground covered – – – – – –

Pass ·········▶

Direction of run ──────▶

Communicate and realign quickly

ACTIVITY: DEFEND AND DEFEND AGAIN

> **CALL OUT** "Communicate who is covering who" • "Come up together in a line" • "If you are set before the pass, then come up quickly"

1 Mark out a 40m x 20m area, split into two 20m square boxes with cones every 5m down the middle. Put four attackers (one with a ball) by one box and three by the other. Put three defenders by the first 5m cone.

2 When you say "go", the four attackers run forward into their box, passing the ball and aiming to score at the far end. The defenders move across to make a tackle.

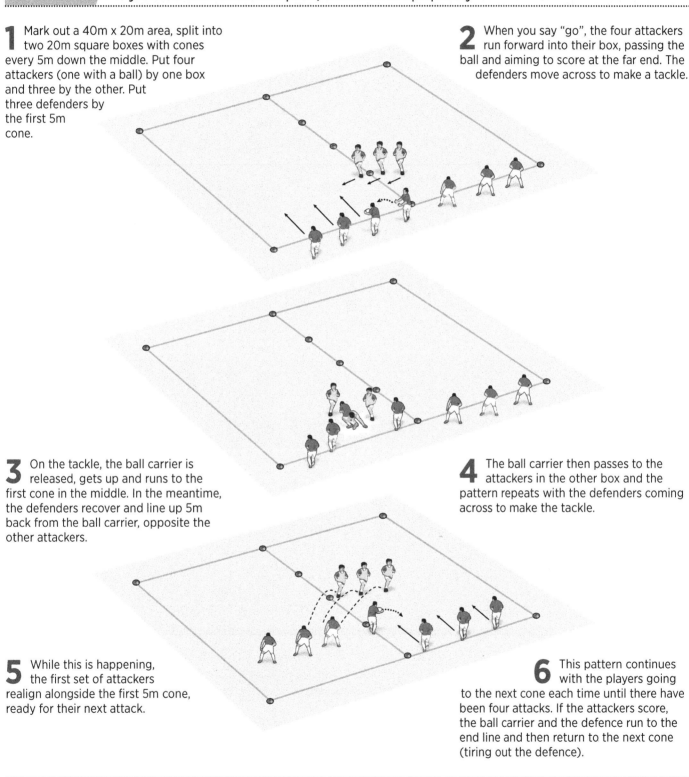

3 On the tackle, the ball carrier is released, gets up and runs to the first cone in the middle. In the meantime, the defenders recover and line up 5m back from the ball carrier, opposite the other attackers.

4 The ball carrier then passes to the attackers in the other box and the pattern repeats with the defenders coming across to make the tackle.

5 While this is happening, the first set of attackers realign alongside the first 5m cone, ready for their next attack.

6 This pattern continues with the players going to the next cone each time until there have been four attacks. If the attackers score, the ball carrier and the defence run to the end line and then return to the next cone (tiring out the defence).

How many players do I need?

You need 10 players for this activity. If you have more, set up another playing area and run another game alongside.

Key

Ground covered	Pass	Direction of run
– – – – –	·····▶	⟶

Fill in defensively and come forward to tackle

ACTIVITY: DEFENCE COMMS

> **CALL OUT** "Move forward together • "Keep communicating that you are in position"
> "Make a side-on tackle – head behind the shorts, tight grip, drive the feet"

1 Set out four cones in a Z-shaped pattern with 2m between each cone. Put a defender at one end and an attacker 2m in front of the Z on the opposite side, between the end and middle cones.

2 Put at least three of these Zs together in a line (this simulates players working together in defence).

3 When you say "go", the defender runs sideways to the next cone and then forward quickly.

4 When the defender reaches the cone in front of him, the attacker moves forward and the defender makes a side-on tackle.

5 Swap attacker and defender and repeat. Then shift cones, so the players are working from the other side.

Starting the defenders from the side of the box allows more side-on tackles to occur

6 Develop with an overload game of three defenders v five attackers in a 20m x 25m area. The defenders run forward from the side and then into the area. As they run into the box, the attackers move forward on your command.

7 Add in different colour cones to vary the entry points of the three defenders so that you can increase or decrease the difficulty of achieving the tackles against an attack.

How many players do I need?
You need at least six players for the first part of the activity and eight for the second part.

Key

Ground covered   **Direction of run**

- - - - - - - - →

© **EasiCoach Rugby Skills Activities**

U13-U16
EVASION

Take a pass under pressure then step away

ACTIVITY: BALANCED RUNNING

CALL OUT "Take short steps just before the ruck pad and then explode away" • "Attack the defender and then step away"

1 Mark out a 15m square area and put a 1m square box inside about 3m from one end. Put an attacker on the line in front of the box and a feeder to the side. Put a ruck pad holder 1m behind the box and position two defenders on the opposite corners of the area.

2 When you say "go", the attacker moves forward and takes a pass from the feeder just before he reaches the box.

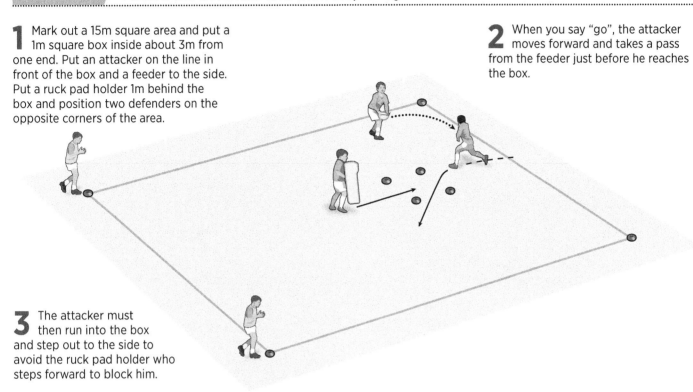

3 The attacker must then run into the box and step out to the side to avoid the ruck pad holder who steps forward to block him.

4 As the attacker steps out of the side of the box, the defender on that side of the area comes forward to stop the attacker getting to the far end of the area.

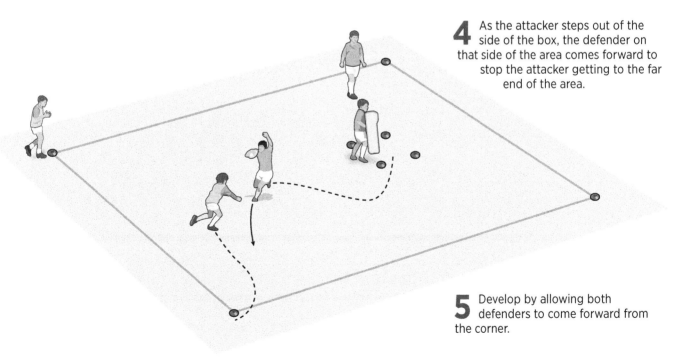

5 Develop by allowing both defenders to come forward from the corner.

How many players do I need?

You need five players for this activity. With more players, line up attackers to come on in quick succession.

Key

Ground covered	Pass	Direction of run
- - - - - - -	· · · · · · · ·▸	⟶

Change the pace of support

ACTIVITY: BACKWARDS TO COME FORWARD

CALL OUT   "Be alert and ready to run forward" • "Keep talking to the players next to you" • "Run onto the ball at pace"

1 Set out three 5m lines of cones 3m apart. Put two ruck pad holders 10m in front of the first two lines and a feeder to the side. Put three attackers with their backs to the lines of cones. Ask them to jog backwards in and out of the cones.

2 When you shout "go", all players come forward. The attackers take a pass from the feeder and aim to beat the ruck pad holders in front of them by getting the ball to the player in space.

3 Develop by changing the distances between attack and defence and making the lines wider apart and the cones more offset.

4 Change the activity round by having three defenders jogging backwards and four attackers coming forward. Play two-handed touch tackling instead of ruck pads.

Defenders can drift or come forward

How many players do I need?
You need six players for the first part of the activity and eight for the second part.

Key

Ground covered	Pass	Direction of run
– – – – – – –	· · · · · · ·▶	———▶

Change line of running to beat defenders

ACTIVITY: CHANGING ANGLES LATE

EasiCoach
RUGBY SKILLS ACTIVITIES

> **CALL OUT** "Make the passes accurate" • "Fix the defender then change your angle" • "Drive off your leg to change direction"

1 Lay out a line of three tackle tubes (or ruck pads) with a 3m gap between each tube. Divide players into groups of three and position a group 6m behind each tube. The tackle tubes are laid out to simulate a defence. Give a ball to the front player of the end group.

2 When you say "go" the front players from each group run forward, with the ball carrier passing to the player outside him as he reaches the tackle tube and the second player passing on to the end player.

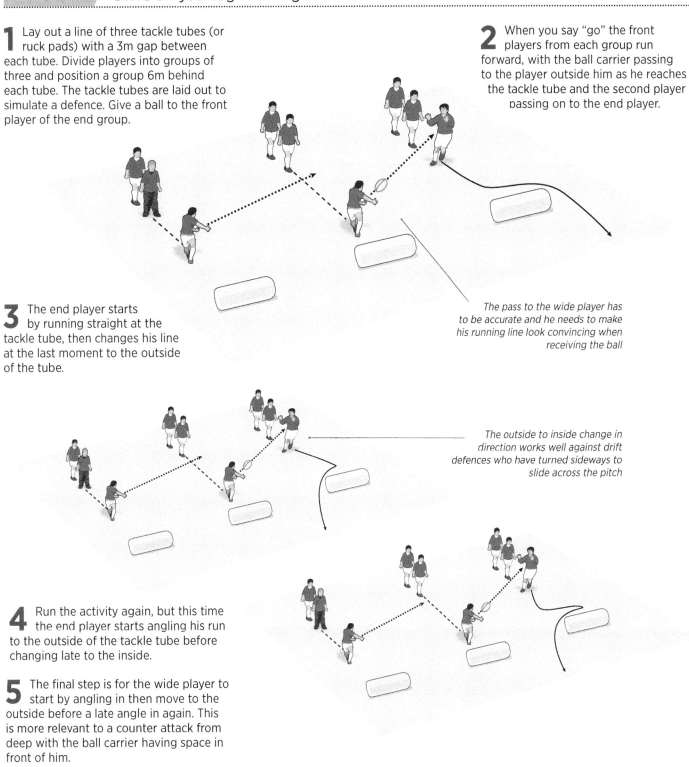

The pass to the wide player has to be accurate and he needs to make his running line look convincing when receiving the ball

3 The end player starts by running straight at the tackle tube, then changes his line at the last moment to the outside of the tube.

The outside to inside change in direction works well against drift defences who have turned sideways to slide across the pitch

4 Run the activity again, but this time the end player starts angling his run to the outside of the tackle tube before changing late to the inside.

5 The final step is for the wide player to start by angling in then move to the outside before a late angle in again. This is more relevant to a counter attack from deep with the ball carrier having space in front of him.

How many players do I need?
Split your players into three groups and line them up behind the tackle tubes.

Key

Ground covered	Pass	Direction of run
– – – – – – –	· · · · · · · ·▸	——————▸

Spin out of a tackle

ACTIVITY: SPIN OUT OF CONTACT

CALL OUT "Spin on the pad of the foot behind the big toe" • "Keep the ball away from the defender"

1 Mark out an 8m x 4m area with a line at 3m. Put an attacker with a ball in the middle of one end of the area and a defender on one knee at the side of the area by the 3m line.

2 When you say "go", the attacker runs forward aiming to make it to the far end of the area and the defender runs in to try and tackle him.

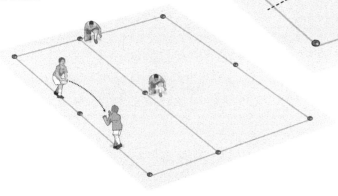

3 The attacker must try to spin before he makes contact with the tackler, so that he avoids the tackler and can run on to the end.

4 The attacker scores 2 points if he makes the far end, and 1 point if he gets over the 3m line. He doubles his score if he uses a spin.

5 Swap the side that the defender starts from and repeat. Then swap attacker and defender.

6 Develop by having two attackers passing the ball between each other in a wider box, with two defenders. When you shout "go", the attacker with the ball aims to beat the defender in his box, with the other two players running across to support their respective team mates.

✓ **Spinning out of a tackle**

Let the players work out their own way to spin out of a tackle. However, it does start with the ball carrier planting one foot near the tackler and then spinning away so that the ball is out of reach of the tackler.

How many players do I need?
You need two for the first part and four for the second part, but this activity moves quickly so line up players to come on.

Key
Ground covered **Direction of run**
- - - - - - - →

© EasiCoach Rugby Skills Activities

U13-U16
HANDLING

Pass correctly then realign

ACTIVITY: PASS AND REALIGN

CALL OUT — "Keep the ball at chest height, but keep it off your chest" • "Reach for the ball – fingers forward and up" • "Follow through in the direction of the pass"

1 Set out a 15m x 5m channel. Put five players in a line along one side of the channel, standing about 3m apart. Put two lines of five players (one in front of the other) on the opposite side. Give a ball to the first player in the front line on one side.

2 When you say "go", the first player runs out and passes to the next player in the line. The players pass down the line to the end player. Players delay their start until after the man next to them has started.

3 Each player in the line must sprint on to the ball then decelerate and pull the pass back in front of the next receiver.

4 All passes must be made within the 5m channel. When the last player in the line has crossed the channel, he hands the ball on to the next group which repeats coming back across the channel.

5 Develop by using a 15m square area divided into three 5m channels. Players start as before, with the first set of passes completed before the first 5m line.

6 The players then stop and realign, then pass back along the line before reaching the second 5m line. After the final pass, the ball carrier sprints to the last 5m line and the other players funnel in behind him. He gives the ball to the end player on the opposite side and the drill is repeated.

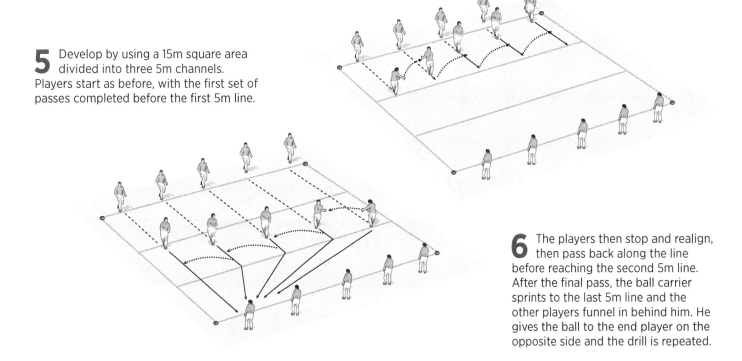

How many players do I need?

You need 15 players to run this activity. If you have more, you can add more lines of five.

Key

Ground covered	Pass	Direction of run
– – – – –	················▶	————▶

Pass the ball behind the first player

ACTIVITY: THE BLOCK PASS

CALL OUT "Turn the shoulders to make the pass" • "Over-emphasise pulling the pass back" • "Outside attacker, be an option to take a pass"

1 Set out two 2m cone gates about 5m apart. Start two attackers 5m in front of the gates and put a feeder just behind the gates to the side.

2 When you say "go", the attackers move forward and the feeder passes to the first attacker who goes through the coned gate in front of him. He then passes back at 45 degrees to the next attacker who runs through the other gate.

The gates force the first attacker to make the pass back at a 45-degree angle.

3 Once the players are used to passing back at 45 degrees, remove the gates and play with two defenders v three attackers. When you say "go", the first attacker takes the pass from the feeder as before.

4 The outside defender decides whether he steps in, towards the first attacker, or out to cover the other attackers. If he steps in, then the first attacker uses the 45-degree pass. If he steps out, then the passer uses a short pass.

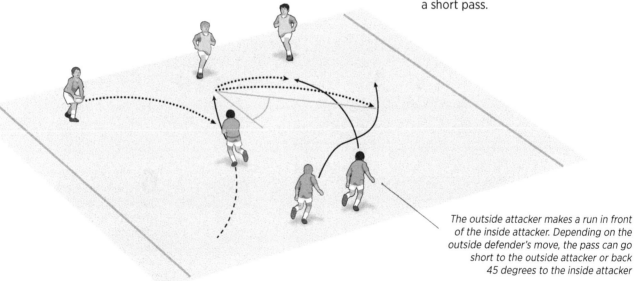

The outside attacker makes a run in front of the inside attacker. Depending on the outside defender's move, the pass can go short to the outside attacker or back 45 degrees to the inside attacker

---

How many players do I need?
You need three players for the first part of the activity and six for the second part.

Key

Ground covered	Pass	Direction of run
– – – – –	·······▶	——▶

Loop behind the receiver to create an extra man

ACTIVITY: LOOPING TO CREATE AN EXTRA MAN

EasiCoach
RUGBY SKILLS ACTIVITIES

CALL OUT "The looping player does not change his running angle until he has passed the ball" • "Pass for the receiver, not to the receiver"

1 Mark out a 10m square area with a 3m channel down one side and a 2m channel down the other (leaving a 5m channel in the middle). Put an attacker with a ball on one side of the 2m channel and another attacker alongside him on the 5m channel then put two defenders on the opposite side facing them.

2 When you say "go", all players move forward. The first attacker must run up the 2m channel until he goes past 3m (use a cone to mark this), at which point he can pass to the attacker in the 5m channel.

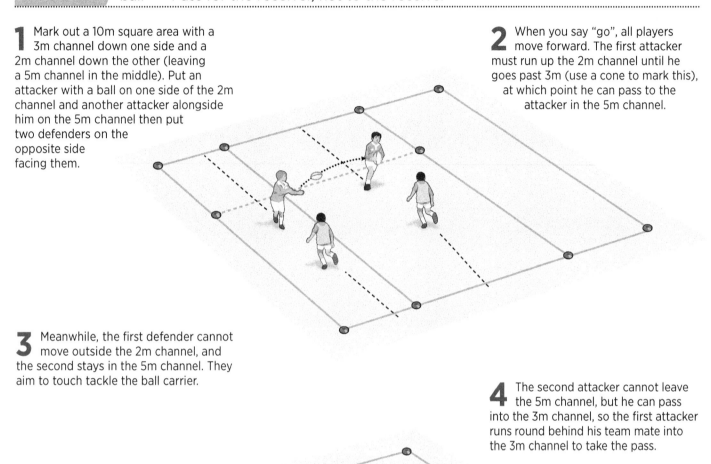

3 Meanwhile, the first defender cannot move outside the 2m channel, and the second stays in the 5m channel. They aim to touch tackle the ball carrier.

4 The second attacker cannot leave the 5m channel, but he can pass into the 3m channel, so the first attacker runs round behind his team mate into the 3m channel to take the pass.

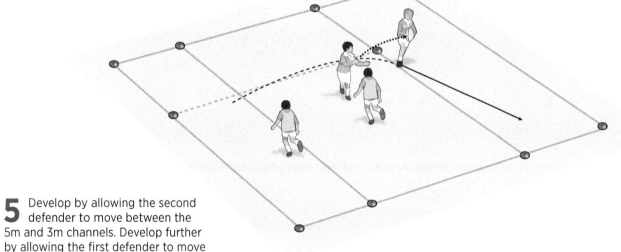

5 Develop by allowing the second defender to move between the 5m and 3m channels. Develop further by allowing the first defender to move between the 2m and 5m channels as well.

How many players do I need?
You need four players for this activity. It's a quick drill, so if you have more, line them up to wait their turn.

Key

Ground covered	Pass	Direction of run
– – – – –	··········	⟶

Run straight, catch and pass to find space

ACTIVITY: RUN STRAIGHT, CATCH AND PASS

EasiCoach
RUGBY SKILLS ACTIVITIES

CALL OUT   "Hands ready to catch the ball"   "Run up the pitch, not across" •
"Keep the ball off the chest"

1 Mark out a 10m x 5m area. Put feeder A on one corner and feeder B on the adjacent corner along one of the long sides. Put three attackers behind the line between the feeders and put two defenders on the opposite side.

2 When you shout out a letter, here "B", that feeder passes a ball to the nearest attacker. He runs forward into the area, passing it to the second attacker who then passes it to the third attacker.

3 In the meantime, the defenders race forward, closing down the first and second attackers.

4 The attackers aim to run straight lines and rely on quick passing and good catching to put the third attacker into space, allowing him to cross the opposite line. The defenders aim to stop the attackers getting their passes away using two-handed touch tackles.

5 Repeat, randomly choosing which side the ball will come from. Rotate players so that they experience attack and defence.

6 Develop by adding another attacker in a 20m x 15m area. Again randomise which side the ball comes from, but now the defenders can choose who they want to defend against.

How many players do I need?
You need seven players for this activity. If you have more, set up another area alongside.

Key

Ground covered	Pass	Direction of run
- - - - - -	·····▶	⟶

Manage the defender and offload the ball

ACTIVITY: MANAGE CONTACT AND OFFLOAD

CALL OUT "Twist and turn your shoulders to keep the ball away from the defender" • "Pass the ball up with the palm of the hand under the ball"

1 Mark out a 5m circle. Put a feeder at the side of the circle, an attacker near the back of the circle and a defender at the front.

2 When you say "go", the feeder passes to the attacker. At the same time the defender comes forward into the circle to challenge the attacker.

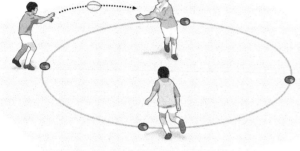

The attacker can move in any direction to avoid the defender but cannot leave the circle.

3 The attacker aims to keep the ball out of the grasp of the defender until the feeder has run around the back of the circle, at which point the attacker offloads the ball to the feeder.

4 Swap the side the feeder starts from and go again, then rotate the players.

✓ **Offloading the ball**

The "hook"

Turn the shoulders, keeping the hand under the ball to hook it to the support player and away from the defender.

The "flick"

Use the arm away from the body, with the palm under the ball to flick the ball away.

How many players do I need?

You need three players for this activity. If you have more players, try to get as many threes practising offloads as space allows.

Key

Ground covered	Pass
- - - - - - - -	·················▸

Pass, run and communicate in a 3v2

ACTIVITY: THE EASIEST 3V2 DRILL EVER

CALL OUT "Attack the defence at pace " • "Move the ball from one to two to one hand to engage a defender from a distance"

1 Five players run forward and pass the ball. You, as the coach, stand nearly opposite the last player.

2 Once the ball reaches the last player, he runs towards you and pops you the ball.

3 The last player and the previous passer run around you and line up to defend.

4 The first three players realign and become attackers, ready to receive the ball from you and launch a 3v2.

5 Playing touch rugby, the attackers use their running, fixing and passing skills, plus offload passing, to beat the players in front of them.

6 Work both left and right, mixing up the players.

How many players do I need?
You need five players for this activity, but you can also play with 4v2, 4v3 or similar combinations.

Key

Ground covered	Pass	Direction of run
– – – – – –	·······▶	——▶

© **EasiCoach Rugby Skills Activities**

Fix a defender by attacking at pace

ACTIVITY: GET READY TO ATTACK

CALL OUT "Hands up to receive the pass" • "Attack at pace" • "Pass for the receiver"

1 Mark out a 20m x 10m area. Put two cones on one long side, 4m and 8m from one corner. Down the centre of the area line up five players, two on yellow cones, two on red and one on white. Put a feeder on the short side of the area facing them.

2 You call either "Yellow" or "Red". The colour called, here "Red", is the defender group. The other colour are the attackers The player on white always joins the attackers.

3 On your call, the defenders run to touch the cones on their try line, while the attackers run to the opposite line.

4 All players then run back into the area. The two defenders can defend against the two inside attackers only, leaving the widest attacker free.

5 The feeder passes to the nearest attacker once the defenders have touched their cones. They all then play out a 3v2 with the free attacker aiming to score over the defenders' line.

6 Develop by allowing defenders to defend against any player so the attack has to decide on choice and time of pass.

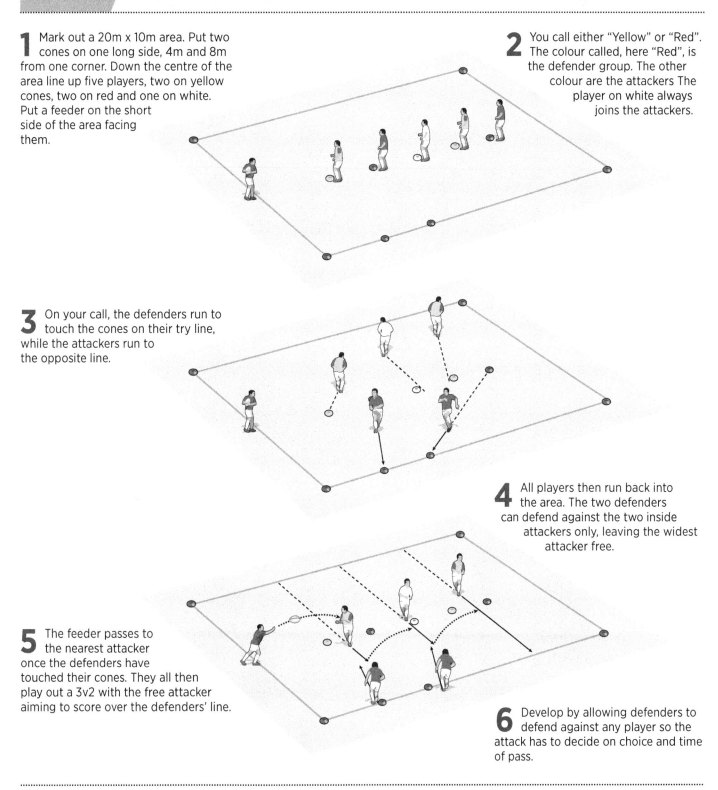

How many players do I need?
You need six players for this activity. If you have more, set up a second playing area and run another game alongside.

Key

Ground covered	Pass	Direction of run
- - - - - - -	· · · · · ▸	⟶

Fend off the tackler or offload the ball

ACTIVITY: FEND AND OFFLOAD

EasiCoach
RUGBY SKILLS ACTIVITIES

CALL OUT ▷ "Twist and turn your shoulders to keep the ball away from the defender" • "Pass the ball up with the palm of the hand under the ball"

1 Mark out a 5m x 3m box 5m in front of an 8m try line. A ball carrier starts at one corner of the box and a defender in the middle of the other side. A support player starts in the middle of the end of the box.

2 When you say "go", the ball carrier aims to score at the far end, but must run inside the cone in front of him first. The defender aims to tackle him – he can cut across the box to make his challenge. The support player follows behind, anticipating the offload.

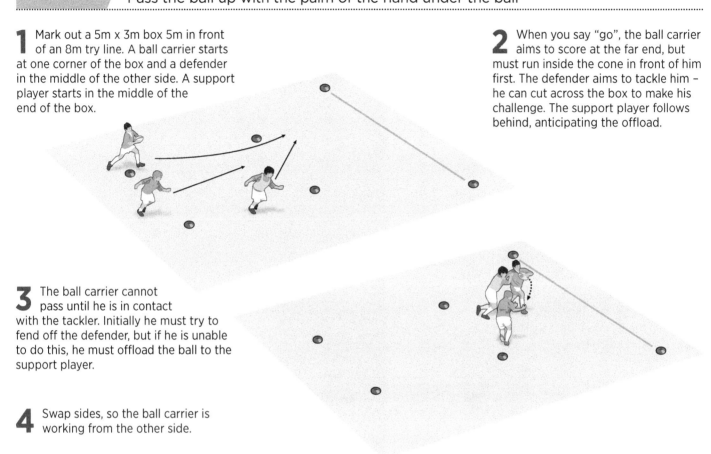

3 The ball carrier cannot pass until he is in contact with the tackler. Initially he must try to fend off the defender, but if he is unable to do this, he must offload the ball to the support player.

4 Swap sides, so the ball carrier is working from the other side.

✓ Fending off a defender

Use a bent arm to push the palm of the hand into the chest or shoulder of the defender

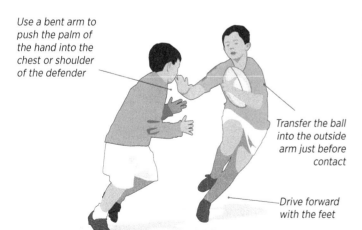

Transfer the ball into the outside arm just before contact

Drive forward with the feet

✓ Offloading the ball

Turn the shoulders, keeping the hand under the ball to hook it to the support player and away from the defender

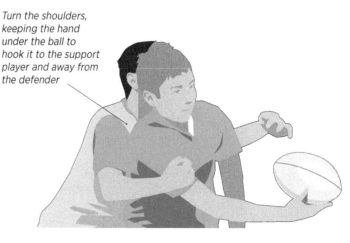

How many players do I need?
You need three players for this activity, but if you have more, get them lining up ready to take their turn.

Key
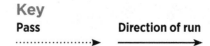
Pass · · · · · · · · ·▶   Direction of run ──────▶

U13-U16

KICKING

Punt the ball accurately through the sweet spot

ACTIVITY: SWEET SPOT KICKING

EasiCoach
RUGBY SKILLS ACTIVITIES

CALL OUT ▸ "Drop the ball onto the foot" • "Kick through the sweet spot" • "Follow through towards target"

1 Initially organise players into groups of four with a ball. Tell them to kick the ball to each other, making sure they use the correct part of the foot (bony) and strike the ball in the "sweet spot".

✓ **Hitting the sweet spot**

Keep the head over the ball and drop it onto the foot, don't throw it up first.

The sweet spot is the area where the ball is at its widest. Aim to drop the ball so that the bony part of the foot connects with the sweet spot.

Kicking the end of the ball will result in a lack of accuracy and distance.

2 When players are confident in their kicking, mark out an area about 40m x 30m. Split each group of four into two pairs and position the pairs so that they're facing each other across the area.

3 Use cones to mark out a 5m circular target zone about 5m in front of each pair. Players take it in turns to kick across the area into the target zone – get them challenging each other to see who can be most consistent in terms of distance kicked and accuracy.

4 If your players are consistent and accurate with their kicking, the next stage is kicking for a wide player who runs and tries to catch the ball. Have a player kicking towards a target zone and another player running from distance to reach the target zone and catch the ball. Again you are looking for accuracy and distance control.

5 A tackle tube can be added into the target areas to create a bit of pressure on the catcher.

How many players do I need?
Split your players into groups of four divided into two pairs. Get as many pairs kicking to each other as space and equipment allow.

Key

Kick ·············▶

Direction of run ──────▶

Take a high ball and run forward

ACTIVITY: TAKING A HIGH BALL

EasiCoach
RUGBY SKILLS ACTIVITIES

CALL OUT "Jump into the catch" • "Challenge the ruck pad holder" • "Hit the ground running"

1 Set out a 15m x 10m area. Put a ruck pad holder in the middle and another ruck pad holder at the end. Line up players on the front end of the area facing the ruck pad holders and place a feeder to the side.

2 When you say "go", the first player comes forward, the feeder throws a ball up into the air and the first player and the ruck pad holder challenge for the ball.

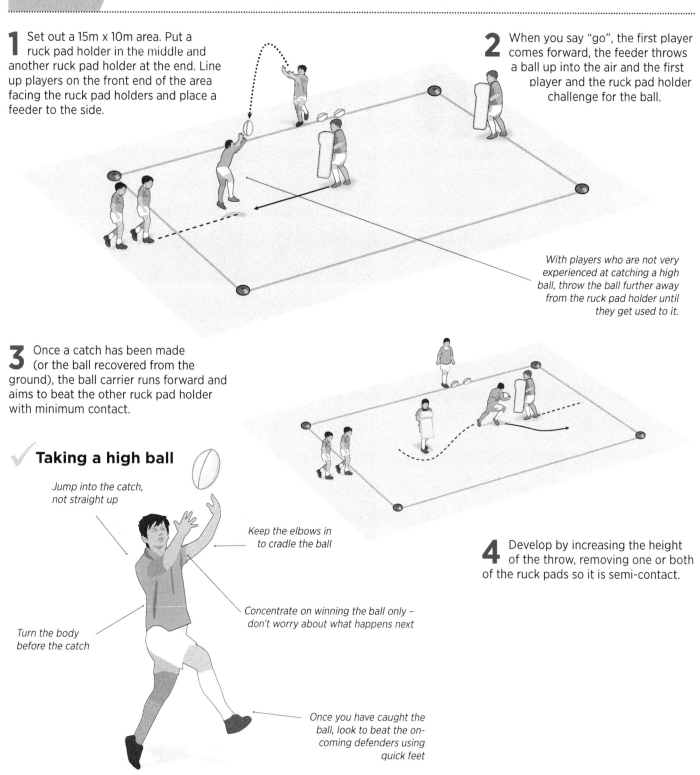

With players who are not very experienced at catching a high ball, throw the ball further away from the ruck pad holder until they get used to it.

3 Once a catch has been made (or the ball recovered from the ground), the ball carrier runs forward and aims to beat the other ruck pad holder with minimum contact.

✓ **Taking a high ball**

Jump into the catch, not straight up

Keep the elbows in to cradle the ball

Turn the body before the catch

Concentrate on winning the ball only – don't worry about what happens next

Once you have caught the ball, look to beat the on-coming defenders using quick feet

4 Develop by increasing the height of the throw, removing one or both of the ruck pads so it is semi-contact.

How many players do I need?
You need at least four players for this activity, but you can line up lots of players and keep the catches coming.

Key

Ground covered	Pass	Direction of run
– – – – –	⋯⋯⋯▶	⟶

Andrew Griffiths

Starting with limited rugby knowledge, Andrew coached his son's team for four years, gaining his Level 1 RFU coaching award, and learning the hard way about grassroots coaching. The experience of managing training for 25 boys and their parents prompted the creation of the EasiCoach Rugby Curriculum. Andrew is the editor of many rugby and soccer coaching manuals, and the managing director of Green Star Media Ltd.

Dan Cottrell

Dan has spent most of his adult life collecting and absorbing the most useful rugby coaching secrets he can find. He is a practising RFU Level 3 Coach, a Welsh Rugby Union Course Leader, head coach for Swansea Schools U15s and a Level 2 referee. Dan played first class rugby at Bath and Bristol and later became Director of Rugby at Cranleigh School in Surrey. He is best known as the editor of the successful free rugby coaching email *Better Rugby Coaching*, which has been published since 2003 and has 80,000 subscribers worldwide.

How EasiCoach Was Created...

EasiCoach Rugby Curriculum™ has been created by the people who publish Rugby Coach Weekly coaching magazine. We have been publishing sports coaching advice for grassroots coaches since 2003.

Covering the key core skills required for consistent player development across five age ranges from U7 to U16, EasiCoach follows the latest mini and youth guidelines on player development and has been approved by senior national coaching development officers.

As a coaching tool aimed at helping beginner coaches, volunteer assistants and helpers, EasiCoach offers a guaranteed programme of skills development activities every season.

EasiCoach is owned by Green Star Media Ltd, which provides informed, easy-to-follow advice for 450,000 rugby, football (soccer) and basketball coaches in more than 80 countries. For more information, please visit www.greenstarmedia.net

Lightning Source UK Ltd.
Milton Keynes UK
UKOW07f1345050917
308628UK00006B/91/P